# CHILDREN'S KNITTING FROM MANY LANDS

Alice Starmore

BELL & HYMAN

LONDON

**Photography by Dennis Thorpe**

Published in 1984 by
Bell & Hyman Limited
Denmark House
37–39 Queen Elizabeth Street
London SE1 2QB

*British Library Cataloguing in Publication Data*
Starmore, Alice
  Children's knitting from many lands.
  1. Children's clothing      2. Knitting—
  Patterns
  I. Title
  646.4′07      TT820
  ISBN 0 7135 2449 9

Designed by Christine Sanderson
Typeset by Inforum Ltd, Portsmouth
Colour separation by Positive Colour, Essex
Produced in Spain by Grijelmo S.A. Bilbao

# Contents

Preface                                      5

Abbreviations and General Notes              6

**1   IN PORT**
**The British Isles**
Fair Isle: *Boy's or girl's pullover*        8
Shetland Lace: *Girl's dress*               12
Aran: *Boy's or girl's jacket*              16
Sanquhar: *Boy's or girl's playsuit,*
        *sweater and beret*                 20
Fisher Gansy: *Boy's or girl's sweater*     25

**2   THE NEXT DOOR GARDEN**
**Western Europe**
Holland: *Girl's dress*                     29
Austria: *Girl's sweater*                   32

**3   OVER THE BORDERS**
**The Baltic**
Estonian Jerkin: *Boy's or girl's*          36
Latvia: *Boy's or girl's waistcoat*         41
Russian Sweater: *Girl's*                   45
Russian Jacket: *Boy's or girl's*           49

**4   THE COLDER COUNTRIES**
**Scandinavia**
Iceland: *Boy's or girl's sweater*          53
Swedish Sweater: *Boy's or girl's*          57
Swedish Pullover: *Boy's*                   60
Norwegian Sweaters: *Boy's or girl's*       63
Norwegian All-in-One Suit: *Boy's or*
                        *girl's*            67
Faroe: *Girl's coat, hat and legwarmers*    72
Finland: *Girl's dress and cardigan*        77

**5   WARMER SEAS**
**The Mediterranean**
France: *Girl's camisole*                   86
Spain: *Girl's blouse*                      89
Italy: *Girl's party dress*                 92

**6   LOOKING EASTWARDS**
**Eastern Europe**
Bulgaria: *Girl's sweater*                  96
Yugoslavia: *Boy's or girl's sweater*      100

**7   FARTHER AND FARTHER**
Arabia: *Boy's or girl's sweater*          104
Inca Jacket: *Girl's*                       108
Bolivian Poncho: *Girl's*                   112
Bolivian Catsuits: *Girl's*                 117

**8   BACK TO THE PARLOUR**
English Lace: *Girl's blouse*              122

Guide to Techniques                        126

# Foreign Lands

Up into the cherry tree
Who should climb but little me?
I held the trunk with both my hands
And looked abroad on foreign lands.

I saw the next door garden lie
Adorned with flowers, before my eye,
And many pleasant places more
That I had never seen before.

I saw the dimpling river pass
And be the sky's blue looking glass;
The dusty roads go up and down
With people tramping into town.

If I could find a higher tree
Farther and farther I should see,
To where the grown-up river slips
Into the sea among the ships,
To where the roads on either hand
Lead onward into fairy land.
Where all the children dine at five,
And all the playthings come alive.

('Foreign Lands' and all other poems quoted
are from *A Child's Garden of Verses* by
Robert Louis Stevenson.)

# Preface

Why children's knitting? Many knitters gain particular enjoyment from knitting for children. A child's garment is smaller and so it is relatively cheaper and faster to produce a really satisfying result. There is also a great deal of scope for variety, and that is the main principle behind this collection of garments.

The collection is intended to include something to suit every child and every knitter. There is variety in style, colour, type and weight of yarn, and in the complexity of the patterns themselves. The Swedish sweater for example, is ideal for someone wishing to try Fair Isle for the very first time, while the Yugoslavian sweater is a challenge for the competent knitter. Above all there is variety in the inspiration behind the collection, for it is literally world-wide, based upon elements of traditional knitting from many countries. Using this book, it should be possible for most knitters to make something really interesting and unusual at a reasonable cost in both time and effort.

The poems of Robert Louis Stevenson perfectly capture the world of children and of foreign lands, and extracts from his verses accompany many of the patterns in this book. I gratefully acknowledge the pleasure he has given to me as a child, to my own children, and to generations of children throughout the world.

Alice Starmore

# Abbreviations and General Notes

## ABBREVIATIONS

**asterisk** * This indicates that the instructions following the symbol are to be repeated a specific number of times

**b** back. Knit or purl into back of stitch(es)

**beg** beginning

**C** contrast shade

**cont** continuity/continuing

**DC** Double crochet

**dec** decrease

**foll** following

**g** gramme

**k** knit

**knit up** Insert the point of the right-hand needle from the front to the back of the fabric, one complete stitch in from the edge. Put the yarn under then over the needle, pull the loop on the needle through the fabric quite loosely, and leave it on the needle, thus forming one stitch

**inc** increase

**m1** make one. Pick up the horizontal thread lying before the next stitch and work into the back of it.

**MB** make bobble. Purl into front and back of next stitch twice. Turn, k4. Turn, p4. Turn, k4. Turn, slip 2nd, 3rd and 4th st over 1st st, then slip 1st st onto right hand needle.

**MK** Make knot thus: k1, p1, k1, p1, k1 loosely into the next st. Then slip the 4th, 3rd, 2nd and 1st stiches, in turn, over the last stitch made, thus completing the knot.

**MS** Main shade

**p** purl

**patt** pattern

**psso** pass slip stitch over. Insert the tip of the left hand needle into the stitch just slipped and draw this stitch over the stitch just knitted, and over the tip of the right hand needle, and off the needle

**rem** remaining

**rep** repeat

**sl** slip. Pass the stitch(es) from the left to the right-hand needle into the stitch to be slipped as if to purl, unless otherwise stated

**ssk** slip, slip, knit. Slip the first and second stitches knitwise, one at a time, then insert the tip of the left hand needle into the fronts of these 2 stitches from the left, and knit them from this position

**st.st.** stocking stitch

**st(s)** stitch(es)

**tbl** through the back of loops

**tog** together

**Tw2F** Twist 2 front by knitting into front of 2nd stitch then front of first stitch on left hand needle, then slipping the 2 sts off the needle together.

**Tw2B** Twist 2 back. As Tw2F, but kintting into the *back* of sts.

**wyf** with yarn forward

**wyb** with yarn back

**yo** yarn over. Take the yarn over the top of the needle once before working the next stitch. If the next stitch is to be knitted, then the yarn is taken over the top of the right-hand needle, to the back; if the next stitch is to be purled, then the yarn is taken over the top of the right hand needle and then under the needle to the front. The yo is counted as a separate stitch on return row.

## TENSION

Tension relates to the number of stitches and rows to a given measurement. The size of every garment is based on this measurement. It is therefore *essential* that you work a tension sample using the correct type of yarn, needle size, and stitch (st.st. or pattern, as stated) before commencing any garment. It is wrong to assume that you will knit to the same tension as that given, and if you are even half a stitch out, your garment could end up as much as 5cm too large or small.

Once you have worked your tension sample, place it on a flat surface and secure it with pins, being careful not to stretch it. Then lay a firm rule across the sample, mark with pins the tension measurement given in the pattern, (e.g. 5cm [2in]) and count the exact number of stitches between the pins. Then measure the rows in the same manner. If your stitches and rows are exactly the same as those given, then it is safe to begin. If you have too few stitches and rows, this means that your tension is too loose. To correct this, work a sample using a smaller size of needle. If you have too many stitches and rows, this means that your tension is too tight. To correct this, work a sample using a larger size of needle.

It is not a reflection on your skill if your tension is looser or tighter than that given in the pattern, and it doesn't matter if you end up using much smaller or larger needles. Once you achieve the given tension, you will knit a perfect garment.

## READING THE CHARTS

The colour designs are set out in charts on graph paper. Each colour is represented by a different symbol on the chart and a key to these symbols is given alongside the chart.

One square represents one stitch and one row of squares represents one complete row of knitting.

The first and every following odd numbered row is worked from right to left, and the second and every following even numbered row is worked from left to right.

The pattern stitches are repeated a specified number of times across the work, and the edge stitches, which are not repeated, are given at each side of the pattern stitches.

Full instructions on using each chart are given in the text. (References to the different numbers of edge stitches needed for different sizes are separated by oblique lines.)

## KNITTING NEEDLES

| Metric (in mm) | |
| --- | --- |
| 9 | 000 |
| 8½ | 00 |
| 8 | 0 |
| 7½ | 1 |
| 7 | 2 |
| 6½ | 3 |
| 6 | 4 |
| 5½ | 5 |
| 5 | 6 |
| 4½ | 7 |
| 4 | 8 |
| 3½ and 3¾ | 9 |
| 3¼ | 10 |
| 2¾ and 3 | 11 |
| 2½ | 12 |
| 2¼ | 13 |
| 2 | 14 |

## CROCHET HOOKS

| Metric (in mm) | |
| --- | --- |
| 7½ | — |
| 7 | 2 |
| 6½ | 3 |
| 6 | 4 |
| 5½ | 5 |
| 5 | 6 |
| 4½ | 7 |
| 4 | 8 |
| 3½ | 9 |
| 3¼ | 10 |
| 2¾ and 3 | 11 |
| 2½ | 12 |
| 2¼ | 13 |
| 2 | 14 |

# 1

# IN PORT
# The British Isles

◇

# Fair Isle

Boy's or Girl's pullover (ages 2–11)

> *The level of the parlour floor*
> *Was honest, homely, Scottish shore;*
> *But when we climbed upon a chair,*
> *Behold the gorgeous East was there!*

Scottish tradition in dazzling colours. An interesting pattern to work.

## SIZES
Approx age: 2–3/6–7/10–11 years
To fit chest: 56/66/76cm (22/26/30in)
Length from top of shoulder: 34/42/49.5cm
(13½/16½/19½in)

## YARN
1/2/2 1oz hanks of 2-ply Shetland jumper
weight yarn in MS
1/2/2 1oz hanks of same in 4th C
1/1/2 1oz hanks of same in 3rd C
1/1/2 1oz hanks of same in 5th C
1 1oz hank in each of first, 2nd, 6th and 7th C
The yarn used in this garment is Jamieson and
Smith 2-ply Shetland jumper weight yarn in
the following shades:
MS – 142 (petrol blue); 1st C – FC7
(tangerine); 2nd C – 1a (natural white); 3rd C
– 129 (flame red); 4th C – 96 (pale yellow);
5th C – 66 (butter yellow); 6th C – FC41 (dark
petrol); 7th C – 121 (gold mix).

## NEEDLES
1 set of 4 2¾mm and 3¼mm needles

## TENSION
16 sts and 16 rows to 5cm (2in) measured over
chart patt, using 3¼mm needles

## BODY
With set of 2¾mm needles and MS, cast on
168/196/224 sts.

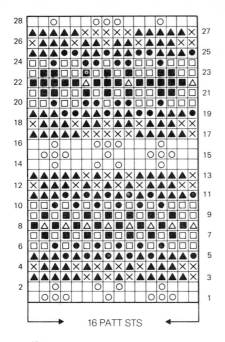

```
28   ○       ○○○        ○
26  ▲▲▲▲×××××▲▲▲▲▲×    27
   ×▲▲▲×▲▲×▲▲×▲▲×▲▲××  25
24  ▲▲▲▲●▲●▲▲●▲▲●▲▲●
   □□□●□□□●□□□●□□□□    23
22  □■□□■□□■□■□□■□□■□
   ■□□□□■□□□△□□■□□■□△  21
20  □□□●□□□●□□□●□□□□
   ▲▲▲●▲▲●▲▲●▲▲▲●▲▲●   19
18  ×▲▲×▲▲×▲▲×▲▲×▲▲××
   ▲▲▲▲×××××▲▲▲▲▲×     17
16   ○       ○○○        ○
   ○○○       ○   ○○○    15
14   ○       ○   ○
   ▲▲▲▲×▲×▲×▲×▲▲▲▲×     13
12  ×▲▲×▲▲×▲×▲×▲▲×▲▲××  11
   ▲▲▲▲●▲●▲◎▲●▲▲●▲▲×
10  □□□●□□□●□□□●□□□□     9
8  ■□△□■□△□■□△□■□△■□△   7
   □□□●□□□●□□□●□□□□
6  ▲▲▲●▲▲●▲▲●▲▲▲●▲▲     5
4  ×▲▲×▲▲×▲×▲×▲▲×▲▲××   3
   ▲▲▲▲×▲×▲×▲×▲▲▲▲×
2   ○       ○   ○        1
   ○○○       ○   ○○○
```

**← 16 PATT STS →**

**Key**

| | |
|---|---|
| | 2nd C (Natural White) |
| ○ | 1st C (Tangerine) |
| × | 3rd C (Flame Red) |
| ▲ | 4th C (Pale Yellow) |
| ● | MS (Petrol Blue) |
| □ | 5th C (Butter Yellow) |
| ■ | 6th C (Dark Petrol) |
| △ | 7th C (Gold Mix) |

Work in corrugated rib as follows:
Rounds 1, 2, 3, and 4: With MS, k2; with 3rd C, p2; rep to end
Rounds 5, 6, 7, and 8: With MS, k2; with 4th C, p2; rep to end
Repeat these 8 rounds until rib measures 5/6/7cm (2/2½/2¾in).

### Next round: increase
With 2nd C (k7, m1) rep to end of round. 192/224/256 sts.
Change to 3¼mm needles and joining in and breaking off colours as required, work the patt from chart, repeating the 16 patt sts 12/14/16 times around body.
Continue in this manner, repeating the 28 patt rows until body measures 21.5/27/31.5cm (8½/10½/12½in) from beg.

### Next round: divide body/ work back
Patt the first 4/5/6 sts of round, then place these sts together with the last 3/4/5 sts of round on a holder, for underarm.
Patt 89/103/117 sts.
** Turn, and working right and wrong side on 2 needles, continue in patt, decreasing 1 st at each end of next and every foll row until 81/93/105 sts remain.
Patt 1 row straight, then decrease 1 st at each end of next and every foll alt row until 71/81/91 sts remain. **
Continue straight in patt until back measures 32.5/39.5/46.5cm (12¾/15½/18¼in) from beg, with right side facing for next row.

### Shape right shoulder
Patt 16/20/24 sts. Place the rem sts on a spare needle.
Turn and patt these sts, decreasing 1 st at beg of first and foll alt rows until 14/17/20 sts remain.
Continue straight to row 8/1/22 of chart patt. Place the sts on a spare needle.

### Shape neck/ left shoulder
With right side facing, place the next (centre back) 39/41/43 sts on a holder for back neck.
Rejoin yarns and patt the rem 16/20/24 sts of left shoulder as right, reversing shaping.

### FRONT
With right side facing, rejoin yarns and patt the first 7/9/11 sts of second underarm and place the sts on a holder.
Patt the rem 89/103/117 sts.
Turn and work as back from ** to **.
Continue straight until front measures 30/36/43cm (11¾/14¼/17in) from beg, with right side facing for next row.

### Shape left shoulder
Patt 19/24/28 sts. Place the rem sts on a spare needle.
Turn and patt these sts, decreasing 1 st at beg of first and every foll alt row until 14/17/20 sts remain.

Continue straight to row 8/1/22 of chart patt. Place the sts on a spare needle.

**Shape neck/ right shoulder**

With right side facing, place the next (centre front) 33/33/35 sts on a holder for front neck. Rejoin yarns and patt the rem 19/24/28 sts of right shoulder as left, reversing shaping.

**FINISHING**

With wrong side out, 3¼mm needles and MS/ 2nd C/MS, cast off shoulder sts together, thus joining back and front.
Sew in loose ends.

**Neck edge**

With right side facing, set of 2¾mm needles, and MS, begin at right shoulder seam and knit up 11/13/14 sts down right back neck, pick up and knit the 39/41/43 sts of back neck, knit up 11/13/14 sts up left back neck, knit up 13/16/17 sts down left front neck, pick up and knit the 33/33/35 sts of front neck, knit up 13/16/17 sts up right front neck. 120/132/140 sts.

With MS and 4th C, work 3/4/4 rounds of corrugated rib. Then with MS and 3rd C, work a further 4/4/5 rounds.
With MS cast off evenly in rib.

**Armhole edgings**

With right side facing, set of 2¾mm needles, and MS, pick up and knit the 7/9/11 sts of underarm, knit up 73/87/97 sts *evenly* around armhole.
Work 7/8/9 rounds of corrugated rib, as neck.
Cast off evenly in rib.
To block and press see Guide to Techniques.

# Shetland Lace

## Girl's dress (ages 8–11)

> *When at home alone I sit,*
> *And am very tired of it,*
> *I have just to close my eyes*
> *To go sailing through the skies –*
> *To go sailing far away*
> *To the pleasant Land of Play;*
> *To the fairy land afar*
> *Where the Little People are.*

A fantasy inspired by the beautiful lace shawls of the Shetland Isles

## SIZES

Approx age: 8–9/10–11 years
To fit chest: 71/76cm (28/30in)
Length from top of shoulder: 76/81cm (30/32in)

## YARN

6/7 1oz hanks of Shetland lace weight yarn
The yarn used in this garment is Jamieson & Smith Shetland 2-ply lace weight yarn in Shade L71.

## NEEDLES

1 pair each 3¼mm and 2¾mm needles
2.50mm crochet hook

## NOTIONS

Shirring elastic

## TENSION

15 sts and 18 rows to 5cm (2in) measured over st.st using 3¼mm needles.

## SKIRT PANELS (make 8)

With 3¼mm needles cast on 4 sts.
Patt as follows:
Row 1: sl1, yo, k1, yo twice, k1, yo, k1–b
Row 2: sl1, p2 tog, p1 k1 into double yo, p2 tog, p1
Row 3: sl1, yo, k4, yo, k1–b
Row 4: sl1, p7
Row 5: sl1, yo, k3, yo twice, k3, yo, k1–b
Row 6: sl1, p2, p2 tog, p1 k1 into double yo, p2 tog, p3
Row 7: sl1, yo, k2, yo twice, k4, yo twice, k2, yo, k1–b
Row 8: sl1, p1, (p2 tog, p1 k1 into double yo, p2 tog) twice, p2
Row 9: sl1, yo, k1, yo, k4, yo twice, k4, yo, k1, yo, k1–b

Row 10: sl1, p3, p2 tog twice, p1 k1 into double yo, p2 tog twice, p4

Row 11: sl1, yo, k4, (yo twice, k4) twice, k4, yo, k1–b

Row 12: sl1, p3, (p2 tog, p1 k1 into double yo, p2 tog) twice, p4

Row 13: sl1, yo, k3, (yo twice, k4) twice, yo twice, k3, yo, k1–b

Row 14: sl1, p2, (p2 tog, p1 k1 into double yo, p2 tog) to the last 3 sts; p3

Row 15: sl1, yo, k2, (yo twice, k4) to the last 3 sts; yo twice, k2, yo, k1–b

Row 16: sl1, p1, (p2 tog, p1 k1 into double yo, p2 tog) to the last 2 sts; p2

Row 17: sl1, yo, k1, yo, k4, (yo twice, k4) to the last 2 sts; yo, k1, yo, k1–b

Row 18: sl1, p3, p2 tog, (p2 tog, p1 k1 into double yo, p2 tog) to the last 6sts; p2 tog, p4

Row 19: sl1, yo, k4, (yo twice, k4) to the last st; yo, k1–b

Row 20: sl1, p3, (p2 tog, p1 k1 into double yo, p2 tog) to the last 4 sts; p4

Row 21: sl1, yo, k3, (yo twice, k4) to the last 4 sts; yo twice, k3, yo, k1–b

Row 22: sl1, p2, (p2 tog, p1 k1 into double yo, p2 tog) to the last 3 sts; p3.

Repeat Rows 15 to 22 until there are 58 sts on needles and finishing with Row 22 (count the sts on wrong side rows only).

Patt as follows:

Row 1: k1–b, k2 tog, k3, yo, k1, (yo twice, k4) to the last 7 sts; yo twice, k1, yo, k3, ssk, k1–b

Row 2: p5, (p2 tog, p1 k1 into double yo, p2 tog) to the last 5 sts; p5

Row 3: k1–b, k2 tog, k5, yo, k1, (yo twice, k4) to the last 9sts; yo twice, k1, yo, k5, ssk, k1–b

Row 4: p7, (p2 tog, p1 k1 into double yo, p2 tog) to the last 7 sts; p7

Row 5: k1–b, k2 tog, k7, yo, k1, (yo twice, k4) to the last 11 sts; yo twice, k1, yo, k7, ssk, k1–b

Row 6: p9, (p2 tog, p1 k1 into double yo, p2 tog) to the last 9 sts; p9

Continue in this manner, working 2 more k sts on each side of k rows, and 2 more p sts on each side of p rows, until your last p row works as follows:

p25, (p2 tog, p1 k1 into double yo, p2 tog) twice, p25.

Next row: k1–b, k2 tog, k25, yo, k1, yo twice, k1, yo, k25, ssk, k1–b

Next row: p27, p2 tog, p1 k1 into double yo, p2 tog, p27

Next row: k1–b, k2 tog, k26, yo, m1, yo, k26, ssk, k1–b

Next row: purl

Now patt as follows:

Row 1: k1–b, k2 tog, k26, yo, k1, yo, k26, ssk, k1–b

Row 2: purl

Repeat these 2 rows and work 14 rows altogether.

**Next row: decrease**

k1–b, k2 tog, k24, k2 tog, yo, k1, yo, ssk, k24, ssk, k1–b

Next row: purl.

Patt 2/4 rows straight.

**Next row: decrease**

k1–b, k2 tog, k23, k2 tog, yo, k1, yo, ssk, k23, ssk, k1–b

Next row: purl.

Patt 2/4 rows straight.

Continue in this manner, decreasing on every 4th/6th row until 31/43 sts remain.

Patt 3 rows straight.

**First size only**

Place the sts on a spare needle.

**2nd size only**

With right side facing, decrease at next and every foll 4th row until 33 sts remain.

Patt 3 rows straight, then place sts on a spare needle.

**BODICE**

With 3¼mm needles, patt across 4 panels as follows:

(k1–b, k2 tog, k 10/11, k2 tog, k1, ssk, k 10/11, ssk, k1–b) 4 times. 108/116 sts.

Purl 1 row.

Change to 2¾mm needles and k1, p1 rib for 7/9 rows.

**Next row: increase**
Rib 3/2, (m1, rib 6/7) to the last 3/2 sts; m1, rib 3/2. 126/133 sts.
Now patt as follows:
Row 1: (right side) * k1, k2 tog, yo, k1, yo, ssk, k1; rep from * to end of row
Row 2: * p2 tog – b, yo, p3, yo, p2 tog; rep from * to end of row
Row 3: * k1, yo, ssk, k1, k2 tog, yo, k1; rep from * to end of row
Row 4: * p2, yo, p3 tog, yo, p2; rep from * to end of row
Repeat these 4 rows until bodice measures 16/18 cm (6¼/7in) from beg of patt, with right side facing for next row.

**Shape armholes**
Keeping continuity of patt as far as possible, cast off 5 sts at beg of next 2 rows.
Cast off 2 sts at beg of next 2 rows.
Decrease 1 st at each end of next 4 rows.
Patt 1 row straight, then decrease 1 st at each end of next and every foll alt row until 90/97 sts remain.
With right side facing, shape neck as follows:
Patt 24/26 sts and place on a spare needle.
Cast off the next 42/45 sts, patt the rem 24/26 sts.
** Turn and keeping continuity of patt as far as possible, decrease 1 st at each end of next and every foll alt row until 18/20 sts remain.
Patt 1 row straight, then decrease 1 st at neck edge only of next and every foll alt row until 7 sts remain.
Continue straight until armhole measures 16.5/18cm (6½/7in).
Cast off all sts **.
With wrong side facing, rejoin yarn to the 24/26 sts from spare needle, and work as

previous from ** to **.
Work another bodice across the rem 4 panels.

**FINISHING**
To block and press see Guide to Techniques.
Join bodices at shoulder seams.

**Neck edge**
With 3¼mm needles cast on 7 sts
Row 1: knit
Row 2: purl
Row 3: sl1 purlwise, k2, yo, k2 tog, yo twice, k2 tog
Row 4: yo, k2, p1, k2, yo, k2 tog, k1
Row 5: sl1 purlwise, k2, yo, k2 tog, k4
Row 6: k6, yo, k2 tog, k1
Row 7: sl1 purlwise, k2, yo, k2 tog, yo twice, k2 tog, yo twice, k2 tog
Row 8: (k2, p1) twice, k2, yo, k2 tog, k1
Row 9: sl1 purlwise, k2, yo, k2 tog, k6
Row 10: k8, yo, k2 tog, k1
Row 11: sl1 purlwise, k2 yo, k2, tog, (yo twice, k2 tog) 3 times
Row 12: (k2, p1) 3 times, k2, yo, k2 tog, k1
Row 13: sl1 purlwise, k2, yo, k2 tog, k9
Row 14: Cast off 7sts, k4, yo, k2 tog, k1.
Repeat rows 3 to 14 until edging fits around neck.
With 2.50mm crochet hook, and beginning at a shoulder seam, attach edging to neck by working DC through first st of edging and neck edge of bodice.
Work a further 2 rounds of DC around neck.
Sew up edging seam at shoulder.
Sew up skirt panels of each piece by stitching k1–b edge sts together.
Sew up side seams.
Work 3 rounds of DC around armholes.
Run 4 rows of shirring elastic round inside of waist rib.

# Aran

### Boy's or girl's jacket (ages 6–13)

> *The sailor sings of ropes and things*
> *In ships upon the seas.*

Typical Aran features in a warm, practical jacket for both boys and girls

**SIZES**
Approx age: 6–7/8–9/10–11/12–13 years
To fit chest: 66/71/76/80cm (26/28/30/31½in)
Length from top of shoulder: 42/46/50/53cm
(16½/18/19¾/21in)
Sleeve seam: 35/38/42/45cm (14/15/16½/17¾in)

**YARN**
8/9/10/11 50g balls of Aran yarn
The yarn used in this garment is Pingouin
Pingostar in Lichen

**NEEDLES**
1 pair each 3¾mm and 4½mm needles

**NOTIONS**
5 buttons

**TENSION**
21 sts and 28 rows to 10cm (4in) measured
over sleeve patt, using 4½mm needles.

**BODY**
(Back and fronts are worked in 1 piece to the
armhole)

With 3¾mm needles cast on 156/168/180/192
sts.
K1, p1 rib for 5/6/6/6cm (2/2½/2½/2½in).

**Next row: increase**
Rib 6/3/10/8, (m1, rib 9/9/8/8) to the last 6/3/
10/8 sts; m1, rib 6/3/10/8. 173/187/201/215 sts.
Change to 4½mm needles and work the wave
and knot patt as follows:
Row 1: (wrong side) k6, * p2, k1, p1, k1, p2,
   k7; rep from * end last rep with k6
Row 2: p4, * p2 tog, k2, p twice into next st,
   k1–b, p twice into next st, k2, p2 tog, p3;
   rep from * end last rep with p4
Row 3: k5, * p2, k2, p1, k2, p2, k5; rep from
   * to end of row
Row 4: p3, * p2 tog, k2, p twice into next st,
   p1, k1–b, p1, p twice into next st, k2, p2
   tog, p1; rep from * end last rep with p3
Row 5: k4, * p2, k3, p1, k3, p2, k3; rep from
   * end last rep with k4
Row 6: p2, k1–b, *p1, k2, p3, MK, p3, k2,
   p1, k1–b; rep from * end last rep with p2
Row 7: k2, p1, * k1, p2, k7, p2, k1, p1; rep
   from * end last rep with k2
Row 8: p2, k1–b, * p twice into next st, k2, p2
   tog, p3, p2 tog, k2, p twice into next st,
   k1–b; rep from * end last rep with p2
Row 9: k2, p1, * k2, p2, k5, p2, k2, p1; rep
   from * end last rep with k2

Row 10: p2, k1–b, * p1, p twice into next st, k2, p2 tog, p1, p2 tog, k2, p twice into next st, p1, k1–b; rep from * end last rep with p2

Row 11: k2, p1, * (k3, p2) twice, k3, p1; rep from * end last rep with k2

Row 12: p2, MK, * p3, k2, p1, k1–b, p1, k2, p3, MK; rep from * end last rep with p2.

Continue in this manner repeating the 12 patt rows until piece measures 24/27/31/33cm (9½/10¾/12¼/13in) from beg, with right side facing for next row.

## Shape right front

K2 tog, patt 38/41/44/47 sts. Place the rem sts on a spare needle.

Turn, and keeping continuity of patt as far as possible, patt to the last 2 sts, p2 tog.

Patt 1 row straight, then continue in patt decreasing 1 st at end (neck edge) of next and every foll alt row until 23/25/27/29 sts rem.

Continue until armhole measures 14.5/15/15/16cm (5¾/6/6/6½in) with wrong side facing for next row.

## Shape shoulder

** Cast off 5/7/6/8 sts, patt to end of row.
Patt 1 row straight.
Cast off 6/6/7/7 sts, patt to end of row.
Rep the last 2 rows once more.
Patt 1 row straight.
Cast off the rem 6/6/7/7 sts. **

## Shape back

With right side facing, rejoin yarn to the sts on spare needle and cast off the next 7/8/9/10 sts (underarm), patt 79/85/91/97 sts. Leave the rem sts on the spare needle.

Turn, and keeping continuity of patt, work straight until armhole measures 14.5/15/15/16 cm (5¾/6/6/6½in), with right side facing for next row.

## Shape shoulders

Keeping continuity of patt, cast off 5/7/6/8 sts at beg of next 2 rows.
Cast off 6/6/7/7 sts at beg of next 6 rows.
Patt 1 row straight, then cast off the rem 33/35/37/39 sts for back neck.

## Shape left front

With right side facing, rejoin yarns to the rem sts on spare needle and cast off the next 7/8/9/10 sts (underarm), patt to the last 2 sts, k2 tog.

Turn, and keeping continuity of patt, decrease 1 st at beg (neck edge) of next and every foll alt row until 23/25/27/29 sts remain.

Continue until armhole measures 14.5/15/15/16cm (5¾/6/6/6½in), with right side facing for next row.

Shape shoulder as right front from ** to **.

## SLEEVES

With 3¾mm needles cast on 36/38/40/42 sts.
K1, p1 rib for 5/5/6/6cm (2/2/2½/2½in).

### Next row: increase

Rib 2/3/2/3, (m1, rib 4) 8/8/9/9 times, m1, rib 2/3/2/3. 45/47/50/52 sts.

Change to 4½mm needles and work sleeve patt as follows:

Row 1: (right side) * k1, p1; rep from * to end/end/last st/last st; k 0/0/1/1

Row 2: knit

Repeat these 2 rows, increasing 1 st at each end of 4th/4th/8th/4th patt row, and every foll 6th row (working increased sts into patt) until there are 73/77/80/84 sts.

Continue straight in patt until sleeve measures 36/39/43/46cm (14¼/15¼/17/18¼in) from beg, with right side facing for next row.

## Shape saddle

Cast off 30/32/32/34 sts at beg of next 2 rows.
Keeping continuity of patt, work the rem 13/13/16/16 sts until saddle corresponds in length with cast off sts of back and front shoulder.
Cast off all sts.

## COLLAR

With 4½mm needles cast on 112/118/124/130 sts.

Work in k1, p1 rib and work shortened rows as follows:

Row 1: Rib 78/82/90/96, turn
Row 2: Rib 44/48/56/62, turn

Continue in rib, but at end of each row work extra sts before turning, as follows:
Work 8 sts extra at end of next 2 rows
Work 6 sts extra at end of next 2 rows
Work 4 sts extra at end of next 4 rows
Work 3 sts extra at end of next 3 rows.

### Next row: increase
Rib 4/3/4/3, (work 3 times into the next st, rib 13/14/15/16) 7 times, work 3 times into the next st, rib 2/0/0/0, work 3 sts extra.
Continue in rib and work 2 sts extra at end of next 6 rows.
Continue in rib across all sts for a further 7 rows.
Cast off loosely and evenly in rib.

### Button band
With 3¾mm needles cast on 8 sts.
K1, p1 rib until band when slightly stretched, fits along front (left for girl, right for boy) from hem to beg of neck shaping. Sew up as you go along.
Cast off all sts.

### Buttonhole band
Cast on as button band and rib for 2 rows.
Make buttonhole as follows:
Row 1: Rib 3, cast off 2, rib 3
Row 2: Rib 3, cast on 2, rib 3.
Continue in rib and make a further 4 buttonholes, last to come 1cm (½in) from top of band, the remainder spaced evenly between. Sew up as you go along.

### FINISHING
To block and press see Guide to Techniques.
Sew up sleeve seams from cuff to within 1cm (½in) of top.
Insert sleeves, stitching each side of saddle to cast off edges of shoulders, and stitching cast off edges of sleeves along armhole edges.
Stitch top ends of sleeve seam to cast off sts underarm.
Stitch cast on edge of collar to neck edges, easing in collar to fit. Stitch ends of collar to cast off edges of front bands.
Sew on buttons to correspond with buttonholes.

# Sanquhar

Boy's or girl's playsuit, sweater and beret (ages 1–3)

> *All the pretty things put by,*
> *Wait upon the children's eye,*
> *Sheep and shepherds, trees and crooks,*
> *In the picture story books.*

One of a number of shepherds' plaid patterns, from around the small town of Sanquhar
on the Scottish border

## SIZES

Approx age: 1–2/2–3 years
To fit chest: 54/56cm (21/22in)
Sweater length from top of shoulder: 27/30cm (10¾/11¾in)
Sleeve seam: 22/24cm (8½/9½in)
Back neck to crotch: 41/46cm (16/18in)
Inside leg: 30/35cm (11¾/13¾in)

## YARN

5 50g balls of DK yarn in D
6/7 50g balls of DK yarn in L
The yarn used in this garment is Emu Shetland
in the following shades:
D – Brecken; L – Bressay

## NOTIONS

2 buttons

## NEEDLES

1 pair each 3¼mm and 4mm needles
1 set of 4 or circular 3¼mm and 4mm needles
for beret
3.50mm crochet hook

## TENSION

25 sts and 25 rows to 10cm (4 in), measured
over chart patt, using 4mm needles.

## PLAYSUIT

### RIGHT LEG

With 3¼mm needles and D, cast on 45/51 sts.
K1, p1 rib for 10cm (4in).

**Next row: increase**

K 0/1, k twice into every st to end of row.
(90/101 sts).
Change to 4mm needles and joining in L,
work the patt from chart, repeating the 22
patt sts 4 times across, and working the first st
and the last 1/12 sts on k rows, and the first
1/12 sts and the last st on p rows as indicated.
Continue in this manner until leg measures
15/20cm (6/8in) from beg of chart patt, with
right side facing for next row.
Keeping continuity of patt, increase 1 st at
each end of next and every foll 3rd row, 8
times (106/117 sts), working increased sts into
patt.
Continue straight until leg measures 25/30 cm
(10/12in) from beg of chart patt, with right
side facing for next row.

### Shape crotch

Cast off 3 sts at beg of next 2 rows.
Decrease 1 st at each end of next 3 rows.

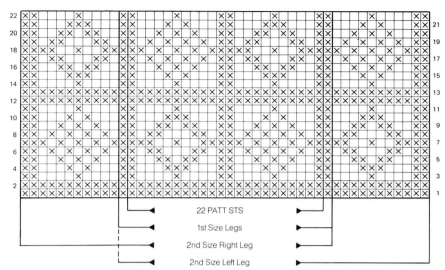

**Key**
☐ D
☒ L

Patt 1 row straight, then decrease 1 st at each end of next and every foll alt row until 88/99 sts remain.
Patt 1 row straight, thus right side should face for next row.
Place these sts on a spare needle.


## LEFT LEG
**1st size:** As right leg, ending on the *same* patt row as right leg.
**2nd size:** As right leg, but reading chart patt as follows:
Repeat the 22 patt sts 4 times across, and working the first 12 sts and the last st on k rows, and the first st and the last 12 sts on p rows as indicated.
End on the *same* patt row as right leg.

### Both sizes – join legs
Keeping continuity of patt, work across all sts of left leg, then across all sts of right leg. (176/198 sts).
Continue straight in patt until piece measures 24/27cm (9½/10¾in) from crotch cast off sts, with right side facing for next row.

### Shape armhole/work left back
Patt 41/46 sts. Place the rem sts on a spare needle.
Turn, and keeping continuity of patt, decrease

1 st at beg of first row, then at the same (armhole) edge of next 2 rows.
Patt 1 row straight, then decrease 1 st at armhole edge of every foll alt row until 36/40 sts remain. Break off L.

### Next row: decrease
With right side facing and D, k2 tog twice, (k2, k2 tog) 8/9 times. (26/29 sts).
Place these sts on a spare needle.

### Armhole/front border
With right side facing, rejoin yarns and cast off the next 6/7 sts.
Keeping continuity of patt, work the next 82/92 sts, leaving the rem sts on a spare needle.

Turn, and decrease 1 st at each end of next 3 rows.
Patt 1 row straight, then decrease 1 st at each end of next and every foll alt row until 72/80 sts remain.

### Next row: decrease
With right side facing and D (k2, k2 tog) 8/9 times, (k2 tog) 4 times, (k2, k2 tog) 8/9 times. 52/58 sts.
Change to 3¼mm needles and with D, purl 1 row.
Join in L and patt front border as follows:

Row 1: With D k1, with L k1; rep to end of
row
Row 2: With D p1, with L p1; rep to end of
row
Repeat these 2 rows until border measures
3cm (1¼in), with right side facing for next row.
Cast off all sts.

### Shape armhole/ work right back
With right side facing, rejoin yarns to the rem
41/46 sts of right back and work as left back,
reversing armhole shaping, and working
decrease row on right side as left back. Place
the rem 26/29 sts on a spare needle.

### FINISHING
To block and press see Guide to Techniques.
Sew up centre seam from crotch to leg join.
Sew up inside leg seams, stitching the first 5cm
(2in) of ankle rib on the right side, for turn up.
Sew up centre back seam.

### Back border
With wrong side facing, 3¼mm needles, and D,
purl 1 row.
Join in L and work as front border.

### Back, front and armhole edgings
With 3.50mm crochet hook, D, and right side
facing, work 2 rows DC along cast off edge of
back and front borders. Then work 2 rows
around each armhole.

### Ties (make 4)
With 3.50mm crochet hook and D, work a
chain 18cm (7in) long. Work 3 rows in DC.
Stitch one tie to each corner of back and front
borders.

## SWEATER

### BACK
** With 3¼mm needles and L, cast on 55/58
sts.
K1, p1 rib for 4.5cm (1¾in).

### Next row: increase
Rib 3/2, (m1, rib 6) 8/9 times, m1, rib 4/2.
64/68 sts.

Change to 4mm needles and work straight in
st.st. until back measures 17/18.5cm (6¾/7¼in)
from beg, with right side facing for next row.

### Shape armholes
Cast off 3 sts at beg of next 2 rows.
Decrease 1 st at each end of next 2 rows.
Work 1 row straight, then decrease 1 st at
each end of next and every foll alt row until
48/52 sts remain. **
Continue straight until armhole measures 5cm
(2in), with right side facing for next row.

### Divide for back neck opening
K 24/26 sts. Place the rem sts on a spare
needle.
Continue straight until armhole measures 10/
11.5cm (4/4½in), with right side facing for next
row.

### Shape shoulder
Cast off 4sts at beg of next and foll alt row.
Work 1 row straight, then cast off 5/6 sts at
beg of next row. Place the rem 11/12 sts on a
length of yarn.
With right side facing, rejoin yarn to sts on
spare needle and work as previous side,
reversing shoulder shaping.

### FRONT
As back from ** to **
Continue straight until armhole measures 8.5/
9.5cm (3½/3¾in), with right side facing for next
row.

### Shape neck
Knit 18/20 sts. Place the next 12 sts on a
length of yarn, and leave the rem sts on a spare
needle.
Turn, and work the sts of left shoulder,
decreasing 1 st at neck edge of first and every
foll alt row 5/6 times. *At the same time*, when
front corresponds in length with back at
shoulder, with right side facing for next row,
cast off shoulder as back.
With right side facing, rejoin yarn and work
the 18/20 sts of right shoulder as left shoulder,
reversing all shapings.

## SLEEVES

With 3¼mm needles and L, cast on 32/34 sts.
K1, p1 rib for 4.5cm (1¾in).

### Next row: increase

Increase 3/4 sts evenly along row. 35/38 sts.
Change to 4mm needles and work in st.st,
increasing 1 st at each end of 4th and every
foll 7th/8th row until there are 47/50 sts.
Continue straight until sleeve measures 22/
24cm (8½/9½in) from beg, with right side facing
for next row.

### Shape top

Cast off 3sts at beg of next 2 rows.
Decrease 1 st at each end of next 2 rows.
Work 1 row straight, then decrease 1 st at
each end of next and every foll
alt row until 23/24 sts remain.
Cast off 3st at beg of next 4 rows.
Cast off the rem 11/12 sts.

## FINISHING

To block and press see Guide to Techniques.
Join back and front at shoulder seams.

### Collar

With 3¼mm needles, L, and beginning at left
back neck, pick up and knit the 11/12 sts from
length of yarn, knit up 9/10 sts down left front
neck, and pick up and knit the first 6 sts from
front neck. (26/28 sts)
K1, p1 rib for 6/8 rows, decreasing/increasing
1 st at beg of last row. (25/29 sts)
Change to 4mm needles, join in D, and patt as
follows:
Row 1: (right side) With L – k1, with D – k1;
    rep to the last st, with L – k1
Row 2: With L – p1, with D – p3; rep to the
    last st, with L – p1
Repeat these 2 rows until collar measures 4cm
(1½in) from beg of patt.
Change to 3¼mm needles, and with D knit 2
rows.
Cast off all sts evenly.
With 3¼mm needles and L, and beginning at
centre front, pick up and knit the rem 6 sts of
front neck, knit up 9/10 sts up right front

neck, and pick up and knit the 11/12 sts of
right back neck.
Work collar as previous side.

### Back neck opening

With 3.50mm crochet hook and L, work 3
rows DC around back neck opening, making
2 buttonholes on the last row, one at top of
collar rib, and one 1.5cm (½in) from bottom of
opening.
Sew up side and sleeve seams.
Insert sleeves.

## BERET

With set of or circular 3¼mm needles, cast on
102 sts.
K1, p1 rib for 2.5cm (1in).

### Next round: increase

(k10, m1) 10 times, k2. (112 sts)
Change to 4mm needles and work 2 rounds
straight.

### Next round: increase

(k11, m1) 10 times, k2. (122 sts)
Work 3 rounds straight.

### Next round: increase

(k12, m1) 10 times, k2. (132 sts)
Work 1 round straight.
Join in D and work the first 13 rows of patt
from chart, repeating the 22 patt sts 6 times
Break off D, and, with L work 1 round
straight.

### Next round: decrease

K19, sl2 – k1 – p2sso; rep 6 times. (120 sts)
K1 round straight.

### 2nd decrease

K17, sl2 – k1 – p2sso; rep 6 times. (108 sts)
Continue to decrease in this manner, working
1 round between decreases, until 12 sts
remain.
Break off yarn and thread through the rem 12
sts several times, and fasten off.

# Fisher Gansy

## Boy's or girl's sweater (ages 2–13)

> *Where shall we adventure, to-day that we're afloat,*
> *Wary of the weather and steering by a star?*
> *Shall it be to Africa, a-steering of the boat,*
> *To Providence or Babylon, or off to Malabar?*

A childs' version of the fishermans' classic. Once a popular and practical garment in many seaports around the British coast.

## SIZES
Approx age: 2–3/4–5/6–7/8–9/10–11/12–13 years
To fit chest: 56/61/66/71/76/79cm (22/24/26/28/30/31in)
Length from top of shoulder: 34/38/42/45/49/52cm (13½/15/16½/17¾/19¼/20½in)
Sleeve seam: 23/27/30.5/34/38/41cm (9/10½/12/13½/15/16in)

## YARN
3/4/4/5/5/6 100g balls of 5-ply guernsey yarn
The yarn used in this garment is Marriner 5-ply guernsey in red and grey

## NEEDLES
1 set each, or circular 2¼mm and 2¾mm needles
NB If using circular needles then 1 pair of 2¾mm needles are also required to work the back and front yoke

## TENSION
16 sts and 20 rows to 5cm (2in) measured over yoke patt, using 2¾mm needles.

## BODY
With 2¼mm needles cast on 144/160/168/180/196/210 sts.
Work in rounds of k1, p1 rib for 4/4/5/5/5/6cm (1½/1½/2/2/2/2½in).

### Next round: increase
(m1, rib 6/8/6/6/7/7) rep to end of round.
(168/180/196/210/224/240 sts)
Change to 2¾mm needles and patt body as follows:

### 1st, 3rd, and 5th sizes only
Work the patt from chart A, repeating the 14 patt sts 12/14/16 times around body. Repeat the 26/24/22 patt rounds 2/3/3 times, then patt rounds 1 to 9/3/19 once more.

### 2nd, 4th, and 6th sizes only
Work the patt from chart C, repeating the 15 patt sts 12/14/16 times around body. Repeat the 6 patt rounds until body measures 20/24/28cm (8/9½/11in) from beg.

### All sizes – work gussets
Increase 1 st at each side of first patt st, continue in patt and work the next 83/89/97/104/111/119 sts, increase 1 st at each side of

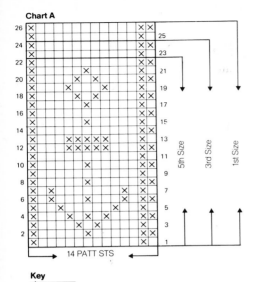

**Chart A**

14 PATT STS

**Key**

| X | Purl |
|---|------|
| | Knit |

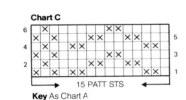

**Chart C**

15 PATT STS

**Key** As Chart A

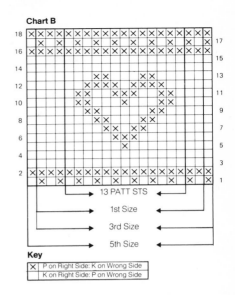

**Chart B**

13 PATT STS

1st Size

3rd Size

5th Size

**Key**

| X | P on Right Side: K on Wrong Side |
|---|------------------------------------|
| | K on Right Side: P on Wrong Side |

**Chart D**

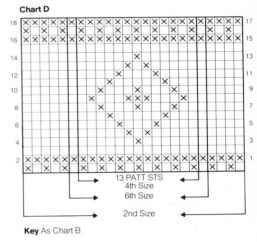

13 PATT STS
4th Size
6th Size

2nd Size

**Key** As Chart B

next st, then patt the rem 83/89/97/104/111/ 119 sts of round, thus dividing the body into 2 equal sections (6/6/7/7/8/8 patt repeats in each section).

Continue in patt, working the gusset sts in st.st. and increasing 1 st into each previous increased st on every 4th round, until there are 11/11/13/13/15/15 sts in each gusset.

**Divide for armholes**

Place the 11/11/13/13/15/15 sts of first gusset on a holder, purl the next 83/89/97/104/111/ 119 sts, place the next 11/11/13/13/15/15 sts of 2nd gusset on a holder, and leave the rem sts on a spare needle.

Turn, and with wrong side facing and using 2 needles, work the 83/89/97/104/111/119 sts of back yoke as follows:

Work the patt from chart B/D/B/D/B/D, repeating the 13 patt sts 6/6/7/8/8/9 times across, and working the first 3/6/3/0/4/1 sts and the last 2/5/3/0/3/1 sts on wrong side rows, and the first 2/5/3/0/3/1 sts and the last 3/6/3/0/4/1 sts on right side rows as indicated, until all 18 rows of chart have been worked.

Patt yoke as follows:

Row 1: (wrong side) purl

Row 2: k2, p2; rep to the last 3/1/1/0/3/3 sts; k these sts

Row 3: purl

27

Row 4: p2, k2; rep to the last 3/1/1/0/3/3 sts; p these sts
Repeat these 4 rows until armhole measures 11.5/12.5/13.5/15/16.5/17cm (4½/5/5½/6/6½/6¾in) from beg, with wrong side facing for next row.

### Shape neck/shoulder

Patt 27/29/32/34/37/40 sts. Place the next 29/31/33/36/38/39 sts on a holder for back neck. Leave the rem sts on a spare needle.
Turn, and decreasing 1 st at neck edge of first row, work ridge patt as follows:
Row 1: purl
Rows 2, 3, and 4: knit
Rows 5 and 6: purl
Leave shoulder sts on a spare needle.
With wrong side facing, rejoin yarn and purl the sts of rem shoulder.
Work ridge patt and decrease as previous shoulder, leaving sts on a spare needle.

### FRONT

Rejoin yarn to the 83/89/97/104/111/119 sts of front and work the chart patt and yoke as back, until armhole measures 10/11/11/12.5/13/13.5cm (4/4½/4½/4¾/5/5¼in) from beg, with wrong side facing for next row.

### Shape neck

Patt 32/34/38/40/44/47 sts. Place the next 19/21/21/24/23/25 sts on a holder for front neck. Leave the rem sts on a spare needle.
Turn and continue in patt, decreasing 1 st at neck edge of the next 3 rows, and every foll alt row until 26/28/31/33/36/39 sts remain. *At the same time*, when yoke patt corresponds in length with back yoke patt, with right side facing, work ridge patt as back shoulder and leave sts on a spare needle.
With wrong side facing, rejoin yarn to the rem shoulder and patt and decrease as previous shoulder, leaving sts on a spare needle.

### Join shoulders

Turn body wrong side out and cast off the sts of each shoulder together, thus forming a ridge.

### Neck

Turn body right side out. With 2¼mm needles and beginning at left shoulder seam, knit up 13/13/15/15/17/17 sts down left front neck, pick up and knit the 19/21/21/24/23/25 sts of front neck, knit up 13/13/15/15/17/17 sts up right front neck, knit up 6 sts down right back neck, pick up and knit the 29/31/33/36/38/39 sts of back neck, knit up 4 sts up left back neck.
K1, p1 rib for 3/3/3/4/4/4cm (1¼/1¼/1¼/1¾/1¾/1¾in).
Cast off loosely and evenly.

### SLEEVES

With right side facing and 2¾mm needles, knit up 72/80/84/92/100/108 sts evenly around armhole, then pick up and knit the 11/11/13/13/15/15 sts of gusset.
Patt the armhole sts as follows:
Round 1: k2, p2; rep to end
Round 2: knit
Round 3: p2, k2; rep to end
Round 4: knit
Repeat these 4 rounds and at the same time work the gusset sts in st.st, decreasing 1 st at each side of first and every foll 4th round until 1 gusset st remains (seam st).
Continue in patt, decreasing 1 st at each side of seam st on every 4th round until sleeve measures 13/15/16/18/20/21 cm (5/5¾/6¼/7/7¾/8¼in).
Continue decreasing on every 4th round and work patt border as follows:
Round 1: purl
Round 2: k1, p1
Round 3: purl
Now work in st.st. and continue to decrease on every 5th round until 45/47/51/51/53/57 sts remain.
If necessary, continue straight in st.st. until sleeve measures 23/27/29/33/37/37cm (9/10½/11½/13/14½/14½in) from beg.
Change to 2¼mm needles, and decreasing 1 st at beg of round, work in k1, p1 rib for 4/4/5/5/5/6cm (1½/1½/2/2/2/2½in).
Cast off evenly in rib.
Press gently on the wrong side (to press see Guide to Techniques).

28

# 2

# THE NEXT DOOR GARDEN

## Western Europe

◇

# Holland

### Girl's dress (ages 3–8)

> *All the names I know from nurse,*
> *Gardener's garters, Shepherd's purse,*
> *Bachelor's Buttons, Lady's smock,*
> *And the Lady Hollyhock.*

Distinctive Dutch lace in pale pastels.

**SIZES**

Approx age: 3–4/5–6/7–8 years
To fit chest 58/63/69 cm (23/25/27 in)
Length from top of shoulder: 56/62/69cm (22/24½/27in)

**YARN**

7/8/9 50g balls of fine cotton yarn in MS
1 50g ball each of same, in 1st, 2nd, and 3rdC
The yarn used in this garment is Pingouin Fil d'Ecosse no.5 in the following shades: MS – Buvard; 1st C – Gris; 2nd C – Cosmos; 3rd C – Ondine

**NEEDLES**

1 pair 2¾mm needles; 2.50mm crochet hook

**TENSION**

16 sts and 22 rows to 5cm (2in) measured over main patt, using 2¾mm needles.

**BACK**

With 2¾mm needles and MS, cast on 169/185/201 sts.
Work 4/4/6 rows garter st (k every row)
Now work main patt as follows:
Row 1: (right side) sl1, * k2–b, p1, k1–b, p1, k2–b, k3, yo, sl1 – k2 tog – psso, yo, k3; rep from * to the last 8 sts; k2–b, p1, k1–b, p1, k2–b, p1
Row 2: sl1, * p2–b, k1, p1–b, k1, p2–b, p9; rep from * to the last 8 sts; p2–b, k1, p1–b, k1, p2–b, p1
Row 3: sl1, * (k1–b, p1) 3 times, k1–b, k2, ssk, yo, k1, yo, k2 tog, k2; rep from * to the last 8 sts; (k1–b, p1) 3 times, k1–b, p1
Row 4: sl1, * (p1–b, k1) 3 times, p1–b, p9; rep from * to the last 8 sts; (p1–b, k1) 3 times, p1–b, p1
Row 5: sl1, * k2–b, p1, k1–b, p1, k2–b, k1, ssk, yo, sl1 – k2 tog – psso, yo, k2 tog, k1;

rep from * to the last 8 sts; k2–b, p1, k1–b, p1, k2–b, p1

Row 6: sl1, * p2–b, k1, p1–b, k1, p2–b, p2, p into front and back of yo from previous row, p1, p into front and back of yo from previous row, p2; rep from * to the last 8 sts; p2–b, k1, p1–b, k1, p2–b, p1

Row 7: sl1, * (k1–b, p1) 3 times, k1–b, (ssk, yo) twice, k1, (yo, k2 tog) twice; rep from * to the last 8 sts; (k1–b, p1) 4 times

Row 8: sl1, * (p1–b, k1) 3 times, p1–b, p9; rep from * to the last 8 sts; (p1–b, k1) 3 times, p1–b, p1.

Repeat rows 1 to 8 and continue until back measures 42/47/52.5cm (16½/18½/20½in) from beg, with right side facing for next row. Decrease as follows:

Row 1: k 1/1/0, (k2 tog, k1) to end/last st/end; k 0/1/0. 114/126/134 sts

Row 2: p 1/2/1, (k2 tog, k3) to the last 3/4/3 sts; k2 tog, k 1/2/1. 91/101/107 sts.

## Shape armholes

Cast off the first 5/6/6 sts, k to end of row. Next row: Cast off the first 5/6/6 sts, p to end of row. 81/89/95 sts.
Knit 1 row. Patt yoke as follows:

Row 1: (wrong side) Knit
Row 2: (k2 tog, yo) to the last st; k1
Row 3: Knit.

Work 11/13/15 rows in st.st.
Repeat these last 14/16/18 rows another 2 times (3 times altogether), then work rows 1 to 3 once again.

## Shape neck

With right side facing, knit 23/25/27 sts and place these sts on a spare needle. Cast off the next 35/39/41 sts, knit the rem 23/25/27 sts. Turn, and work the 23/25/27 sts of shoulder: Work 10/12/14 rows st.st, then with wrong side facing for next row, work the first 3 rows of yoke patt once.
Now work 6 rows garter st and cast off all sts. With wrong side facing, rejoin yarn to the rem 23/25/27 sts and work as before.

## FRONT

As back.

## Vandyke edging

Cast on 7 sts. Row 1: Knit. Row 2: Purl.
Row 3: sl1 purlwise, k2, yo, k2 tog, (yo) twice, k2 tog
Row 4: yo, k2, p1, k2, yo, k2 tog, k1
Row 5: sl1 purlwise, k2, yo, k2 tog, k4
Row 6: k6, yo, k2 tog, k1
Row 7: sl1 purlwise, k2, yo, k2 tog, (yo) twice, k2 tog, (yo) twice, k2 tog
Row 8: (k2, p1) twice, k2, yo, k2 tog, k1
Row 9: sl1 purlwise, k2, yo, k2 tog, k6
Row 10: k8, yo, k2 tog, k1
Row 11: sl1 purlwise, k2, yo, k2 tog, (yo twice, k2 tog) 3 times
Row 12: (k2, p1) 3 times, k2, yo, k2 tog, k1
Row 13: sl1 purlwise, k2, yo, k2 tog, k9
Row 14: Cast off 7 sts, k4, yo, k2 tog, k1.
Repeat rows 3 to 14.

With 2¾mm needle and 1st C, work 4 edgings for back and front shoulders, sewing on edgings with MS as you go along. Sew on by oversewing through the first st of edging and the loop formed by the k row underneath the holes in yoke patt.
With 2nd C work 2 edgings to fit along the k row beneath the next set of holes on front and back, and sew on as before.
With 3rd C work 2 edgings to fit along the k row beneath the next set of holes on front and back, and sew on as before.
With 1st C, work 2 edgings to fit along the k row beneath the next set of holes on front and back, and sew on as before.
With MS work 2 edgings to fit along the k row beneath the bottom set of holes on front and back, and sew on as before.

## FINISHING

Join back and front at shoulder seams. With MS work 2 edgings to fit evenly along armhole edges, sewing up as you go along. and leaving yoke edgings free. Sew up side seams.
With 2.50mm crochet hook and MS, work 3 rows of DC along each side of neck, leaving yoke edgings free. Stitch ends of DC to front and back neck. With crochet hook and MS, work 3 rows of DC along cast off sts of armholes. Stitch ends of DC to armhole edge, behind Vandyke edging.

# Austria

## Girl's sweater (ages 4–11)

> *All by myself I have to go,*
> *With none to tell me what to do —*
> *All alone beside the streams*
> *And up the mountain-sides of dreams.*

Patterns from the Austrian Tyrol are reminiscent of those from Aran, with cables, bobbles and rich textures. The embroidered flowers are a typical finishing touch.

## SIZES
Approx age: 4–5/6–7/8–9/10–11 years
To fit chest: 61/66/71/76cm
(24/26/28/30in)
Length from top of shoulder: 38/42/46/49cm
(15/16½/18/19¼in)
Sleeve seam: 27/31/34/38cm
(10¾/12¼/13½/15in)

## YARN
7/8/9/10 50g balls of Aran yarn
Oddments of DK yarn in red, white and green
The yarn used in this garment is Marriner Regency Bainin in French Navy

## NEEDLES
1 pair each 3¾mm and 4½mm needles
1 darning needle

## TENSION
21 sts and 28 rows to 10cm (4in) measured over Broken Rib patt, using 4½mm needles.

## PATTERN PANELS

### Broken rib
Row 1: (right side) * K1, p1; rep from * to the last st, k1
Row 2: Knit
Repeat these 2 rows.

### Tyrolean fern
Row 1: (right side) k1, Tw2F, Tw2B, k1, p5, Tw2B, k1, MB, k1, Tw2F, p5, k1, Tw2F, Tw2B, k1
Row 2: k1, p4, k6, p7, k6, p4, k1
Row 3: k1, Tw2B, Tw2F, k1, p4, Tw2B, k5, Tw2F, p4, k1, Tw2B, Tw2F, k1
Row 4: k1, p4, k5, p9, k5, p4, k1
Row 5: k1, Tw2F, Tw2B, k1, p3, Tw2B, k1, MB, k3, MB, k1, Tw2F, p3, k1, Tw2F, Tw2B, k1
Row 6: k1, p4, k4, p11, k4, p4, k1
Row 7: k1, Tw2B, Tw2F, k1, p2, Tw2B, k9, Tw2F, p2, k1, Tw2B, Tw2F, k1
Row 8: k1, p4, k3, p13, k3, p4, k1
Row 9: k1, Tw2F, Tw2B, k1, p1, Tw2B, k1, MB, k7, MB, k1, Tw2F, p1, k1, Tw2F, Tw2B, k1

Row 10: k1, p4, k2, p15, k2, p4, k1
Row 11: k1, Tw2B, Tw2F, k1, Tw2B, k13, Tw2F, k1, Tw2B, Tw2F, k1
Row 12: k1, p4, k1, p17, k1, p4, k1
Row 13: k1, Tw2F, Tw2B, k3, MB, k11, MB, k3, Tw2F, Tw2B, k1
Row 14: As row 12
Row 15: k1, Tw2B, Tw2F, k19, Tw2B, Tw2F, k1
Row 16: As row 12.
Repeat rows 1 to 16.

## BACK
** With 4½mm needles, cast on 67/75/79/83 sts.
Knit 2 rows, then work Broken Rib patt until piece measures 6/7/7/8cm (2½/2¾/2¾/3in) from beg, with wrong side facing for next row.
Decrease as follows:
K 2/0/3/0, (k2 tog, k 4/4/3/3) 10/12/14/16 times, k2 tog, k 3/1/4/1. 56/62/64/66 sts.
Change to 3¾mm needles and k1, p1, rib for 3/3/4/4cm (1¼/1¼/1¼/1¾in), with wrong side facing for next row.
Increase as follows:
Rib 3/1/4/1, (m1, rib 5/5/4/4) 10/12/14/16 times, m1, rib 3/1/4/1. 67/75/79/83 sts.
Change to 4½mm needles, and place the pattern panels as follows:
Work Broken Rib over the first 19/23/25/27 sts, work Tyrolean Fern over the next 29 sts, and work Broken Rib over the last 19/23/25/27 sts.
Continue in this manner, working every row of each pattern panel, until back measures 25/28/31/32.5cm (10/11/12/12¾in) from beg, with right side facing for next row.

## Shape armholes
Keeping continuity of patt, cast off 3/3/4/4 sts at beg of next 2 rows.
Decrease 1 st at each end of next 2 rows.
Patt 1 row straight, then decrease 1 st at each end of next and every foll alt row until 51/55/57/59 sts remain. **
Continue straight in patt until armhole measures 13/14/15/16.5cm (5/5½/6/6½in) from beg, with right side facing for next row.

## Shape shoulders
Keeping continuity of patt, cast off 4/5/5/5 sts at beg of next 2 rows.
Cast off 5 sts at beg of next 4 rows.
Place the rem 23/25/27/29 sts on a length of yarn for back neck.

## FRONT
As Back from ** to **.
Continue straight in patt until armhole measures 10/11/12/13cm (4/4¼/4¾/5in) from beg, with right side facing for next row.

## Shape left shoulder
Patt 18/20/20/21 sts. Place the rem sts on a spare needle.
Turn, and keeping continuity of patt, decrease 1 st at neck edge of next and every foll alt row 4/5/5/6 times. *At the same time*, when front corresponds in length with back at shoulder, with right side facing for next row, shape shoulder as follows:
Cast off 4/5/5/5 sts, patt to end of row.
Patt 1 row straight, then cast off 5 sts and patt to end of next row.
Repeat the last 2 rows once more, casting off the last 5 sts on the last row.

## Front neck
With right side facing, place the next (centre) 15/15/17/17 sts on a length of yarn for front neck.

## Right shoulder
With right side facing, rejoin yarn to the rem 18/20/20/21 sts and work as Left shoulder, reversing all shapings.

## SLEEVES
With 3¾mm needles, cast on 34/36/38/40 sts.
K1, p1 rib for 4/5/6/6cm (1½/2/2½/2½in).

## Next row: increase
Rib 1/3/3/5, (m1, rib 4/5/4/3) 8/6/8/10 times, m1, rib 1/3/3/5. 43/43/47/51 sts.
Change to 4½mm needles and place the pattern panels as follows:

Work Broken Rib over the first 7/7/9/11 sts, work Tyrolean Fern over the next 29 sts, and work Broken Rib over the last 7/7/9/11 sts. Continue in this manner, working every row of each pattern panel, and increasing 1 st at each end of 8th/6th/6th/6th row and every foll 12th row, until there are 51/55/59/63 sts (work all increased sts into patt).
Continue straight in patt until sleeve measures 27/31/34/38cm (10¾/12¼/13½/15in) from beg, with right side facing for next row.

### Shape top

Keeping continuity of patt, cast off 3/3/4/4 sts at beg of next 2 rows.
Patt 2 rows straight, then decrease 1 st at each end of next and every foll alt row until 29/31/31/33 sts remain.
Then decrease 1 st at each end of next and every foll row until 15/17/17/19 sts remain.
Cast off 3/3/3/4 sts at beg of next 2 rows
Cast off the rem 9/11/11/11 sts.

### FINISHING

The pieces of this garment do not require pressing.
With oddments of DK yarn and darning needle, embroider flowers and leaves in daisy stitch on all Tyrolean Fern panels, as photograph.
Join back and front at right shoulder.
To press seams see Guide to Techniques.

### Collar

With right side facing and 3¾mm needles, knit up 9/10/10/11 sts down left front neck, pick up and knit the 15/15/17/17 sts of front neck, knit up 9/10/10/11 sts up right front neck, pick up and knit 23/25/27/29 sts of back neck. 56/60/64/68 sts.
K1, p1 rib for 2.5/2.5/3/3cm (1/1/1¼/1¼in), with right side of garment facing for next row.
Increase as follows:
Rib 4/6/4/6, (m1, rib 4) 12/12/14/14 times, m1, rib 4/6/4/6. 69/73/79/83 sts.
Change to 4½mm needles and work Broken Rib until patt measures 5/5/6/6cm (2/2/2½/2½in) with right side of patt facing for next row.
Knit 3 rows.
Cast off loosely and evenly.
Join left shoulder/collar seam.
Join side and sleeve seams.
Insert sleeves.

# 3
# OVER THE BORDERS
## The Baltic

◇

# Estonian Jerkin

Boy's or girl's jerkin (ages 2–11)

> *Over the borders, a sin without pardon,*
> *Breaking the branches and crawling below,*
> *Out through the breach in the walls of the garden,*
> *Down by the banks of the river we go.*

The banks of the Baltic Sea are the home of literally thousands of patterns for gloves and mittens. Here is one of them, on a casual jerkin for either boy or girl.

## SIZES
Approx age: 2–3/4–5/6–7/8–9/10–11 years
To fit chest: 56/61/66/71/76cm (22/24/26/28/30in)
Length from top of shoulder: 34/38/42/46/50cm (13½/15/16½/18/19¾in)

## YARN
2/2/3/3/4 2oz hanks of 3-ply Shetland yarn in MS
1/2/2/2/3 2oz hanks of same in C
The yarn used in this garment is Jamieson and Smith 3-ply Shetland in the following shades:
MS – H51; C – H1a

## NEEDLES
1 pair each 3¾mm and 4½mm needles

## NOTIONS
6/6/7/8/9 buttons

## TENSION
25 sts and 25 rows to 10cm (4in) measured over chart patt, using 4½mm needles.

## BACK
With 3¾mm needles and C, cast on 68/72/80/84/88 sts.
K2, p2 rib for 4 rows.
Break off C, and with MS rib until piece measures 5/5/5.5/6/6cm (2/2/2¼/2½/2½in) from beg.

**Next row: increase**
Rib 4/1/4/7/4, (m1, rib 5/5/6/5/5), to the last

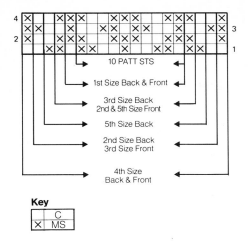

4
3
2
1

10 PATT STS

1st Size Back & Front

3rd Size Back
2nd & 5th Size Front

5th Size Back

2nd Size Back
3rd Size Front

4th Size
Back & Front

**Key**

| | C |
|---|---|
| ✕ | MS |

4/1/4/7/4 sts; m1, rib 4/1/4/7/4. 81/87/93/99/105 sts.
Change to 4½mm needles and joining in C, work the patt from chart, repeating the 10 patt sts 8/8/9/9/10 times across, and working the first 0/3/1/4/2 sts and the last 1/4/2/5/3 sts on knit rows, and the first 1/4/2/5/3 sts and the last 0/3/1/4/2 sts on p rows as indicated.
Continue in this manner, repeating the 4 patt rows until back measures 20/23/25.5/28/31cm (8/9/10/11/12¼in) from beg, with right side facing for next row.

**Shape armholes**
Keeping continuity of patt, cast off 4/4/4/5/5 sts at beg of next 2 rows.
Decrease 1 st at each end of next and every foll row until 67/71/75/79/83 sts remain.
Patt 1 row straight, then decrease 1 st at each end of next and every foll alt row until 59/61/63/67/69 sts remain.
Continue straight in patt until armhole measures 14/15/16.5/18/19cm (5½/6/6½/7/7½in) from cast off row, with right side facing for next row.

**Shape shoulders**
Keeping continuity of patt, cast off 6/5/5/6/6 sts at beg of next 2 rows.
Cast off 5/6/6/6/6 sts at beg of next 4 rows
Place the rem 27/29/31/33/35 sts on a length of yarn for back neck.

**LEFT FRONT**
With 3¾mm needles and C, cast on 34/36/40/42/44 sts.
K2, p2 rib for 4 rows (1st and 4th sizes having a k2 at each end of right side rows).
Break off C, and with MS continue in rib until piece measures 5/5/5.5/6/6cm (2/2/2¼/2½/2½in) from beg.

**Next row: increase**
Rib 2/3/2/3/2, (m1, rib 5/5/6/6/5) to the last 2/3/2/3/2 sts; m1, rib 2/3/2/3/2. 41/43/47/49/53 sts.
Change to 4½mm needles and joining in C, work the patt from chart, repeating the 10 patt sts 4/4/4/4/5 times across, and working the first 0/1/3/4/1 sts and the last 1/2/4/5/2 sts on k rows, and the first 1/2/4/5/2 sts and the last 0/1/3/4/1 sts on p rows as indicated.
Continue in this manner repeating the 4 patt rows until piece measures 4/4.5/5/5.5/6cm (1½/1¾/2/2¼/2½in) from beg of chart patt, with right side facing for next row.

**Divide for pocket openings**
Patt 20/21/23/24/26 sts. Place the rem 21/22/24/25/27 sts on a spare needle. Turn, and keeping continuity of patt, work these 20/21/23/24/26 sts for a further 6/7.5/8.5/9/10cm (2½/3/3¼/3½/4in), ending with wrong side facing for next row. Place the sts on a spare needle.
With right side facing, rejoin yarns to the 21/22/24/25/27 sts on spare needle, and keeping continuity of patt, work straight until piece corresponds in length with previous piece, ending on the *same* patt row.

**Join pieces**
With wrong side facing, patt across all 41/43/47/49/53 sts.
Continue in patt until front measures 20/23/25.5/28/31cm (8/9/10/11/12¼in) from beg, with right side facing for next row.

**Shape armhole**
Keeping continuity of patt, cast off 4/4/4/5/5 sts at beg of next row.
Then decrease 1 st at cast off edge of next and

every foll row until 33/35/37/39/41 sts remain
Patt 1 row straight, then decrease 1 st at same
edge of next and every foll alt row until 30/31/
32/34/35 sts remain.
Continue straight in patt until front measures
31/35/38/42/46cm (12¼/13¾/15/16½/18¼in) from
beg, with right side facing for next row.

## Shape neck
Patt to the last 4/4/5/5/6 sts and place these sts
on a safety pin.
Turn and patt the rem sts.
Next row: Patt to the last 3/3/3/4/4 sts and
place these sts on a safety pin.
Turn and patt the rem sts.
Then decrease 1 st at neck edge of next and
every foll row until 18/19/20/21/21 sts remain.
Decrease at neck edge of next and foll alt
row, decreasing 2/2/3/3/3 sts altogether. *At the
same time*, when front corresponds in length
with back at armhole, with right side facing
for next row, shape shoulder as follows:
Cast off 6/5/5/6/6 sts at beg of next row
Patt 1 row straight, then cast off 5/6/6/6/6 sts
at beg of next and foll alt row.

## RIGHT FRONT
As left front, but reversing armhole, neck,
and shoulder shapings.

## Pocket borders
With 3¾mm needles and MS, and right side
facing, knit up 16/18/20/22/24 sts along pocket
opening (left side of opening for left front,
and right side of opening for right front).
K2, p2 rib for 6/6/6/8/8 rows (2nd and 4th
sizes having a k2 at each end of first and foll
alt rows).
Break off MS, and with C rib a further 2
rows.
Cast off evenly.

## Pocket linings
With wrong side facing, 4½mm needles, and
MS, knit up 15/17/19/21/23 sts along rem side
of pocket openings, beginning at top end of
opening for left front, and bottom end of
opening for right front.

Purl 1 row, then working in st.st increase 1 st
at bottom edge of every row until there are
20/23/25/28/31 sts.
Work 6/6/8/8/8 rows straight, then decrease 1
st at each end of next and every row until
8/9/11/14/15 sts remain.
Cast off evenly.

## FINISHING
To block and press see Guide to Techniques.
Stitch ends of pocket borders to fronts.
Pin pocket linings to fronts and catchstitch in
position.
Join back and fronts at shoulder seams.

## Armhole borders
With right side facing, 4½mm needles and MS,
knit up 67/71/79/83/87 sts along armhole edge.
Knit 1 row, then patt as follows:
Row 1: (right side) with C – k3, * sl1 purlwise
    wyb, k3; rep from * to end of row
Row 2: With C – k3, *sl1 purlwise wyf, k3;
    rep from * to end of row
Row 3: With MS – k1, * sl1 purlwise wyb, k3;
    rep from *, end sl1 purlwise wyb, k1
Row 4: With B – k1, * sl1 purlwise wyf, k3;
    rep from *, end sl1 purlwise, k1.
Repeat rows 1 to 4 and continue in patt for
14/14/16/16/18 rows.
Cast off evenly.

## Collar
With right side facing, 4½mm needles, and
MS, and beginning at right front neck edge,
pick up and knit the 7/7/7/8/9/10 sts from safety
pin, knit up 8/10/10/10/10 sts up right front
neck edge, pick up and knit the 27/29/31/33/35
sts of back neck, knit up 8/10/10/10/10 sts
down left front neck edge, pick up and knit
the 7/7/7/8/9/10 sts from safety pin. 57/63/67/71/
75 sts.
Knit 1 row.
Join in C and work in patt until collar
measures 12.5/13/14/15/16cm (5/5¼/5½/6/6¼in),
with wrong side facing for next row.
Cast off all sts evenly.
Fold collar in half, wrong side out, and sew
up each end.

Turn collar right side out and catchstitch cast off end neatly around neck.

Sew up side and armhole border seams.

Fold armhole borders in half to the inside and catchstitch neatly in position.

**Button band**

With 3¾mm needles and MS, cast on 6/6/8/8/8 sts.

K2, p2 rib until band, when slightly stretched, fits along front opening (left for girl, right for boy) from hem to neck edge. Sew up as you go along.

**Buttonhole band**

As button band with the addition of 6/6/7/8/9 buttonholes, first to come 1 cm (¼in) from hem, last to come 1cm (¼in) from top of band, and the rest evenly spaced between.

To make buttonhole: Rib 2, k2 tog, yo, rib 2/2/4/4/4.

Sew on buttons.

# Latvia

### Boy's or girl's waistcoat (ages 4–13)

Quiet shades for the small, regular Baltic patterns on this waistcoat.
Spot the Fair Isle connection!

## SIZES

Approx age: 4–5/6–7/8–9/10–11/12–13 years
To fit chest: 61/66/71/76/80 cm (24/26/28/30/
31½in)
Length from top of shoulder: 38/42/46/49/
52cm (15/16½/18/19¼/20½in)

## YARN

2/3/3/4/4 50g balls of DK yarn in MS
1 50g ball in each of 1st, 2nd and 3rd C
The yarn used in this garment in Emu
Supermatch DK in the following shades:
MS – Fawn; 1st C – Amber; 2nd C – Grey;
3rd C – Pale Green

## NEEDLES

1 pair each 3¼mm, 4mm, and 4½mm needles

## NOTIONS

5/5/5/6/6 buttons

## TENSION

23 sts and 30 rows to 10cm (4in) measured
over st.st. using 4mm needles.

## BACK

With 3¼mm needles and MS, cast on 65/71/76/
81/86 sts.
k1, p1 rib for 2 rows (1st, 2nd and 4th sizes

having a k st at each end of right side rows)
Join in contrast yarns and k1, p1 rib as
follows:
* 2 rows 1st C/2 rows MS/2 rows 2nd C/2 rows
MS/2 rows 3rd C/2 rows MS; rep from * until
rib measures 5/5/6/6/6cm (2/2/2½/2½/2½in).

**Next row: increase**
Continuing in colour sequence, rib 1/4/3/2/1,
(m1 rib 7) to the last 1/4/3/2/1 sts; m1, rib
1/4/3/2/1. 75/81/87/93/99 sts.
Change to 4½mm needles and joining in and
breaking off colours as required, work the 25
rows of patt from chart, repeating the 24 patt
sts 3/3/3/3/4 times across, and working the
first 1/4/7/10/1 sts and the last 2/5/8/11/2 sts on
k rows, and the first 2/5/8/11/2 sts and the last
1/4/7/10/1 sts on p rows as indicated.
Change to 4mm needles and continue straight
in st.st until back measures 23.5/26/29/30.5/
32.5cm (9¼/10¼/11¼/12/12¾in) from beg, with
right side facing for next row.

**Shape armholes**
Cast off 4 sts at beg of next 2 rows.
Cast off 2 sts at beg of next 2 rows.
Decrease 1 st at each end of the next 4 rows.
Work 1 row straight, then decrease 1 st at
each end of next and every foll alt row until
47/51/55/59/63 sts remain.
Continue straight until armhole measures
14.5/16/17/18.5/19.5cm (5¾/6¼/6¾/7¼/7¾in) with
right side facing for next row.

41

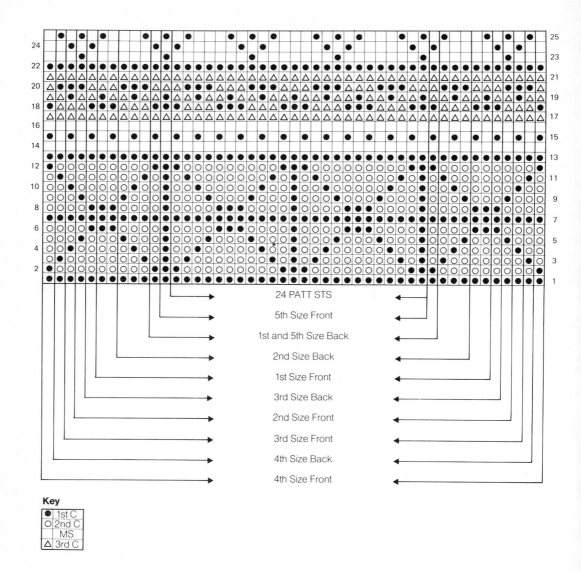

**Key**

| | |
|---|---|
| ● | 1st C |
| ○ | 2nd C |
| | MS |
| △ | 3rd C |

## Shape shoulders

Cast off 5/5/6/6/7 sts at beg of next 2 rows.
Cast off 5/6/6/7/7 sts at beg of next 2 rows.
Cast off the rem 27/29/31/33/35 sts for back neck.

## RIGHT FRONT

With 3¾mm needles and MS, cast on 32/35/37/41/43 sts.
Work in k1, p1 rib and colour stripes as back for 5/5/6/6/6cm (2/2/2½/2½/2½in).

## Next row: increase

Continuing in colour sequence, rib 2/2/1/3/1, (m1, rib 7/6/7/7/8) to the last 2/3/1/3/2 sts; m1, rib 2/3/1/3/2. 37/41/43/47/49 sts.
Change to 4½mm needles and joining in and breaking off colours as required, work the 25 rows of patt from chart, repeating the 24 patt sts 1/1/1/1/2 time(s) across, and working the first 6/8/9/11/0 sts and the last 7/9/10/12/1 sts on k rows, and the first 7/9/10/12/1 sts and the last 6/8/9/11/0 sts on p rows as indicated.
Change to 4mm needles and continue straight

42

in st.st. until front corresponds in length with back at armhole, with wrong side facing for next row.

### Shape armhole/neck
Cast off 4 sts, p to the last 2 sts; p2 tog.
Work 1 row straight, then cast off 2sts at beg of next row.
Then decrease 1 st at armhole edge of the next 4 rows. *At the same time*, decrease 1 st at neck edge of 3rd row from first decrease, and every foll 3rd row. Work 1 row straight, then decrease 1 st at armhole edge of next and every foll alt row 4/5/5/6/7 times altogether. *At the same time*, continue to decrease at neck edge on every 3rd row.
Then continue straight at armhole edge and decrease at neck edge as before, until 10/11/12/13/14 sts remain.
Continue straight until armhole corresponds in length with back at shoulder, with wrong side facing for next row.

### Shape shoulder
Cast off 5/5/6/6/7 sts, work to end of row.
Work 1 row straight, then cast off the rem 5/6/6/7/7 sts.

### LEFT FRONT
As right, reversing all shapings.

### FINISHING
To block and press see Guide to Techniques
Join back and fronts at shoulders.

### Armhole bands (make 2)
With 3¼mm needles and MS, cast on 6/6/6/8/8 sts.
k1, p1 rib until band when slightly stretched, fits around armhole.
Sew up as you go along.

### Front/neck band
With 3¼mm needles and MS, cast on 8/8/8/10/10 sts.
Working in k1, p1 rib make 5/5/5/6/6 buttonholes, first to come 1cm (½in) from beg of band, last to come 1cm (½in) below beg of neck shaping, the rem spaced evenly between. Sew up as you go along, sewing up on the right front for girls, and the left front for boys.
Continue in rib until band fits round neck and down rem front, sewing up as you go along.
Sew up side seams.
Sew on buttons to correspond with buttonholes.

# Russian Sweater

## Girl's sweater (ages 8–11)

> But yonder, see! apart and high,
> Frozen Siberia lies; where I,
> With Robert Bruce and William Tell,
> Was bound by an enchanter's spell.

Warmth with a difference. A distinctive sweater for a girl, in a typical Russian pattern.

## SIZES
Approx age: 8–9/10–11 years
To fit chest: 71/76cm (28/30in)
Length from top of shoulder: 46/49cm (18/19½in)
Sleeve seam 39/43cm (15½/17in)

## YARN
9/10 50g balls of chunky yarn in MS
5/6 50g balls of same in C
The yarn used in this garment is Emu
Finlandia in the following shades:
MS – Jarvi; C – Hango

## NEEDLES
1 pair each 5mm and 5½mm needles

## TENSION
18 sts and 18 rows to 10cm (4in) measured
over chart A patt, using 5½mm needles.

## BACK AND FRONT (2 pieces alike)
With 5mm needles and MS, cast on 50/56 sts.
Change to C, and working in stripes of 2 rows
C/2 rows MS, knit all rows until piece

measures 4cm (1½in) with wrong side facing
for next row.

**Next row: increase**
k 1/4, (m1, k3) 16 times, m1, k 1/4. 67/73 sts.
Change to 5½mm needles and work the patt
from Chart A, repeating the 10 patt sts 6/7
times across, and working the first 3/1 sts and
the last 4/2 sts on k rows, and the first 4/2 sts
and the last 3/1 sts on p rows as indicated.
Continue in this manner until piece measures
26/27cm (10¼/10¾in) from beg, with right side
facing for next row.

**Shape for yoke**
Patt 33/36 sts. Place the rem sts on a spare
needle.
Turn, and keeping continuity of patt,
decrease 1 st at beg of next and *same* edge of
every foll row until 2 sts remain.
k2 tog and fasten off.
With right side facing, rejoin yarns to the rem
sts and cast off the first (centre) st, then
keeping continuity of patt work to end of
row.
Turn, and decrease 1 st at end of next and
*same* edge of every foll row until 2 sts remain.
k2 tog and fasten off.

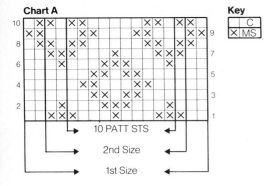

**Chart A**

**Key**

C
× MS

10 PATT STS

2nd Size

1st Size

## SLEEVES

With 5mm needles and MS, cast on 24/27 sts.
Change to C and knit in stripes as back and
front until piece measures 4cm (1½in), with
wrong side facing for next row.

### Next row: increase

k1, k twice into every st to end of row. 47/53
sts.
Change to 5½mm needles and work the patt
from Chart A, repeating the 10 patt sts 4/5
times across, and working the first 3/1 sts and
the last 4/2 sts on k rows, and the first 4/2 sts
and the last 3/1 sts on p rows as indicated.
Continue in this manner until sleeve
measures 39/43cm (15½/17in) from beg.
Break off MS and with C cast off all sts.

## BACK YOKE

With 5½mm needles and MS, cast on 1 st.
Purl 3 times into this st, then working in st.st
increase 1 st at each end of every row as
shown on chart B, until there are 7 sts (row 4,
chart B).
Then join in C and work the patt from chart
B, increasing 1 st at each end of every row as
indicated.
Continue in this manner working 36/38 rows
altogether. 71/75 sts.
Break off C and with MS cast off all sts.

## FRONT YOKE

Work as back yoke to row 24.

## Shape neck

With wrong side facing and working row 24,
patt 23 sts (including increased st).
Turn and decrease at neck edge of every row,
and continue to increase at outside edge, as
indicated in chart B.
Continue in this manner to end of row 36/38.
Break off C and with MS cast off all sts.
With wrong side facing, rejoin yarn and cast
off the first (centre) st. Work the rem sts as
indicated in chart B, then cast off all sts.

## Yoke edgings

With right side facing, 5½mm needles, MS,
and beginning at left shoulder of back yoke,
knit up 38/40 sts to centre of yoke.
Knit 4 rows, increasing 1 st at each end of first
and 3rd row.
Cast off evenly.
With right side facing and beginning at centre
yoke, knit up and work right back yoke
edging as left.
Work edgings on front yoke as back.

## Collar

With 5mm needles and MS, cast on 60 sts.
Knit 9 rows.
Cast off evenly.

## FINISHING

To block and press see Guide to Techniques.
Join back and front yokes at shoulders.
Pin back and front to yokes, overlapping the
garter st edging, and oversew each seam
evenly on the inside.
Pin collar around neck, crossing left front
over right.
Stitch loosely and evenly in position.
Sew on sleeves, placing centre top of sleeves
at shoulder seams.
Sew up side and sleeve seams.

## Tassles

With C, cut 2 lengths of yarn 10cm (4in) long
for each tassle. Place 1 at each corner then
place tassles along edgings at even intervals of
approx 2½cm (1in).

**Chart B**

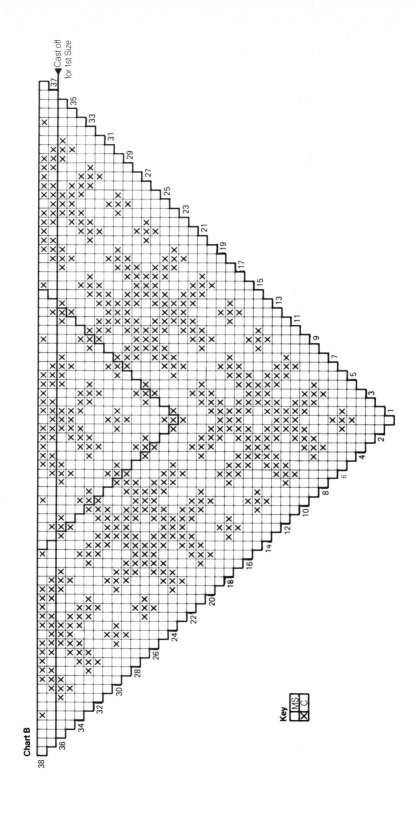

Cast off
for 1st Size

Key

| MS | |
|----|----|
| C | × |

48

# Russian Jacket

## Boy's or girl's jacket (ages 6–11)

Patterns from Russian mittens, worked in the autumnal shades favoured by Russian knitters

**SIZES**

Approx age: 6–7/8–9/10–11 years
To fit chest: 66/71/76cm (26/28/30in)
Length from top of shoulder: 37/40/44cm
(14½/15¾/17¼in)
Sleeve seam: 34/38/42cm
(13½/15/16½in)

**YARN**

7/7/8 50g balls of chunky yarn in MS
1 50g ball of same in each of 1st C, 2nd C and
3rd C
The yarn used in this garment is Emu
Finlandia in the following shades:
MS – Rauma; 1st C – Hango; 2nd C – Kimita;
3rd C – Turku

**NEEDLES**

1 pair each 4½mm and 5½mm needles

**NOTIONS**

1 open-ended zip fastener

**TENSION**

15 sts and 21 rows to 10cm (4in), measured
over st.st. using 5½mm needles.

**BACK/SIDES**

With 4½mm needles and MS, cast on
66/72/78 sts.

Work in garter st (k every row) for 4/5/5cm
(1½/2/2in).

**Next row: increase**

K 1/4/0, (m1, k 9/7/7) 7/9/11 times, m1, k
2/5/1. 74/82/90 sts.
Change to 5½mm needles and work straight in
st.st. until piece measures 21/23/26cm (8¼/9/
10¼in) from beg, with right side facing for
next row.

**Divide for right armhole/side**

K 8/9/10. Leave the rem sts on a spare needle.
Turn and continue straight in st.st, until right
armhole measures 16/17/18cm (6¼/6¾/7in),
with wrong side facing for next row.

**Shape shoulder**

Cast off 4/4/5 sts at beg of next row.
Work 1 row straight, then cast off the rem
4/5/5 sts.

**Back**

With right side facing, rejoin MS and cast off
the next 2 sts from spare needle, k the next
54/60/66 sts. Leave the rem 10/11/12 sts on the
spare needle.
Turn, and continue straight in st.st until back
corresponds in length with right side at
shoulder shaping, with right side facing for
next row.

**Shape shoulders**

Cast off 4/4/5 sts at beg of next 2 rows.
Cast off 4/5/5 sts at beg of next 2 rows.

49

**Chart A**

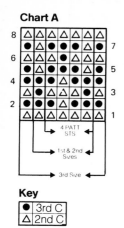

4 PATT STS
1st & 2nd Sizes
3rd Size

**Key**

| ● | 3rd C |
|---|-------|
| △ | 2nd C |

**Chart B**

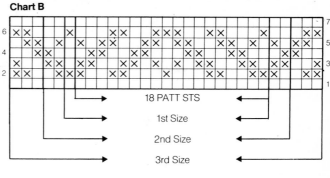

18 PATT STS
1st Size
2nd Size
3rd Size

**Key**

| × | MS |
|---|------|
|   | 1st C |

Cast off 11/12/13 sts at beg of next 2 rows. Place the rem 16/18/20 sts on a holder (back neck).

### Left armhole/side

With right side facing, rejoin MS and cast off the next 2 sts from spare needle, k the rem 8/9/10 sts.

Turn and continue straight in st.st. until left armhole corresponds in length with back at shoulder shaping, with right side facing for next row.

Shape shoulder as right side.

### LEFT FRONT

With right side facing, MS, and 5½mm needles, knit up 53/57/63 sts *evenly* along left edge, beginning at shoulder and ending at top of garter st welt.

Then with MS knit 1 row. Break off MS. Join in 1st C and knit 2 rows. Break off 1st C. Join in 2nd and 3rd C and work the patt from chart A, repeating the 4 patt sts 13/14/15 times across, and working the first 0/0/1 sts and the last 1/1/2 sts on k rows, and the first 1/1/2 sts and the last 0/0/1 sts on p rows as indicated.

Keeping continuity of patt, cast on 1 st at shoulder edge of 3rd patt row.

Work the rem rows of chart A, then break off 2nd and 3rd C.

With MS work 2 rows straight, casting on 1 st at shoulder edge of first row.

Join in 1st C and work the patt from chart B, repeating the 18 patt sts 3 times across, and working the first 0/2/5 sts and the last 1/3/6 sts on k rows, and the first 1/3/6 sts and the last 0/2/5 sts on p rows as indicated. *At the same time*, when left front corresponds in width with left back, along shoulder shapings, with wrong side facing for next row, shape neck as follows:

Patt to the last 6 sts, place these sts on a safety pin.

Turn, and keeping continuity of patt, decrease 1 st at neck edge of next 4/5/5 rows. *At the same time*, when all 7 rows of chart B have been worked, break off 1st C and continue in MS, working 4/5/5 rows straight after the last neck decrease. Leave the sts on a spare needle.

### RIGHT FRONT

With right side facing, MS, and 5½mm needles, knit up 53/57/63 sts *evenly* along right edge, beginning at top of garter st welt, and ending at shoulder. Work as left front reversing all shapings. Leave sts on a spare needle.

### LEFT FRONT WELT

With right side facing, 4½mm needles and MS,

knit up 16/17/18 sts evenly along bottom front edge. Knit 1 row.

Work in garter st stripes of 2 rows each of the contrast yarns, until welt corresponds in length with back/sides welt, with wrong side facing for next row.

Cast off firmly and evenly.

## RIGHT FRONT WELT

As left front welt.

## SLEEVES

With 4½mm needles and MS, cast on 26/28/30 sts.

Work in garter st for 4/5/5cm (1½/2/2in).

### Next row: increase

K 2/3/1, (m1, k 3/3/4) 7 times, m1, k 3/4/1. 34/36/38 sts.

Change to 5½mm needles and work in st.st, increasing 1 st at each end of 4th and every foll 7th/8th/9th row until there are 48/52/54 sts.

Continue straight in st.st. until sleeve measures 34/38/42cm (13½/15/16½in) from beg, with right side facing for next row. Cast off.

## FINISHING

To block and press see Guide to Techniques. Join back and fronts at shoulder seams.

## Neck

With right side facing, 4½mm needles and MS, knit up 6/7/7 sts around right front neck, pick up and knit the 6 sts from right safety pin, pick up and knit the 16/18/20 sts from back neck, pick up and knit the 6 sts from left safety pin, and knit up 6/7/7 sts around left front neck. 40/44/46 sts.

Knit 1 row.

Break off MS and work in garter st stripes of 2 rows each of contrast yarns, until collar measures 4cm (1½in), with wrong side facing for next row.

## Left front opening

With right side facing, 4½mm needles and 1st C, knit up 7 sts along collar edge, pick up and knit the sts from spare needle, knit up 7/9/9 sts along welt edge.

Work in stripes as collar until edging measures 3cm (1¼in), with wrong side facing for next row.

Cast off evenly.

## Right front opening

As left front opening.

Sew up sleeve seams.
Insert sleeves.
Sew up left and right front welt seams.

# 4

# THE COLDER COUNTRIES
## Scandinavia

◇

# Iceland

Boy's or girl's sweater (ages 2–13)

> *Summer fading, winter comes –*
> *Frosty mornings, tingling thumbs,*
> *Window robins, winter rooks,*
> *And the picture story books.*

A sweater to suit all ages, in suitably icy colours. Seamless and easy to work.

**SIZES**
Approx age: 2–3/4–5/6–7/8–9/10–11/12–13 years
To fit chest: 56/61/66/71/76/80cm (22/24/26/28/30/31½in)
Length from back neck: 31/35/39/43/46/48cm (12¼/13¾/15½/17/18/19in)
Sleeve seam: 23/27/31/34/38/40cm (9/10½/12¼/13½/15/15¾in)

**YARN**
4/4/5/5/6/6 50g balls of chunky yarn in MS
2/2/2/3/3/3 50g balls of same in 1st C
1/2/2/2/2/2 50g balls of same in 2nd C

**NEEDLES**
1 set or circular needles in 5mm and 6½mm

**TENSION**
15 sts and 20 rows to 10cm (4in), measured over st.st. using 6½mm needles.

**SLEEVES**
With set or circular 5mm needles and 1st C, cast on 22/24/26/28/30/32 sts.
K1, p1 rib in rounds until cuff measures 4/4/5/5/6/6cm (1¾/1¾/2/2/2½/2½in).

Increase as follows:
**1st size** (k3, m1; k4, m1) 3 times, k1. (28 sts)
**2nd size** (k3, m1) 8 times. (32 sts)
**3rd size** (k4, m1; k5, m1) twice (k4, m1) twice. (32 sts)
**4th size** (k3, m1; k4, m1) 4 times. (36 sts)
**5th size** (k5, m1) 6 times. (36 sts)
**6th size** (k4, m1) 8 times. (40 sts)

**Chart A**

PATT STS

**Key**

| | MS |
|---|---|
| ● | 1st C |
| ✕ | 2nd C |

**Chart B**

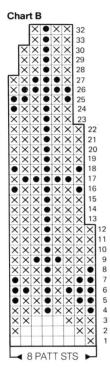

◄ 8 PATT STS ►

## All sizes

Change to 6½mm needles and joining in colours as required, work the 3 rounds of patt from chart A, repeating the 4 patt sts 7/8/8/9/9/10 times around sleeve.

Break off contrast yarns, and with MS work 3 rounds in st.st..

### Next round: increase

K1, m1, k to the last st of round, m1, k1.
Continue in st.st, working 5/7/7/9/9/11 rounds straight and increasing as before on every 6th/8th/8th/10th/10th/12th round, until there

are 40/42/44/46/48/50 sts.
Continue straight until sleeve measures 23/27/31/34/38/40cm (9/10½/12¼/13½/15/15¾in) from beg, ending at end of round.

### Next round

K 4/4/5/5/6/6 and sl these sts onto a length of yarn, k 32/34/34/36/36/38 sts and place on a spare needle, sl the rem 4/4/5/5/6/6 sts onto a length of yarn.

## BODY

With 5mm needles and 1st C, cast on 76/84/90/98/104/108 sts.
K1, p1 rib in rounds until piece measures 4/4/5/5/6/6cm (1¾/1¾/2/2/2½/2½in)
Increase as follows:
**1st and 3rd sizes** (k6, m1; k7, m1) 4/6 times, (k6, m1) twice. (88/104 sts)
**2nd and 4th sizes** (k7, m1) to end of round. (96/112 sts)
**5th size** (k6, m1; k7, m1) to end of round. (120 sts)
**6th size** (k6, m1; k7, m1) 7 times, (k8, m1; k9, m1). (124 sts)
Change to 6½mm needles, and joining in colours as required, work the 3 rounds of patt from chart A, repeating the 4 patt sts 22/24/26/28/30/31 times around body.
Break off contrast yarns and continue straight in MS and st.st. until body measures 18/20/23½/26/27½/29cm (7/8/9¼/10¼/10¾/11½in) from beg, ending at end of round.

### Yoke

Next round: K 4/4/5/5/6/6 and sl these sts onto a length of yarn, k 36/40/42/46/48/50, k the 32/34/34/36/36/38 sts of 1st sleeve, sl the next 8/8/10/10/12/12 sts of body onto a length of yarn, k 36/40/42/46/48/50, k the 32/34/34/36/36/38 sts of 2nd sleeve, sl the rem 4/4/5/5/6/6/ sts of body onto a length of yarn. 136/148/152/164/168/176 sts.

### 2nd and 4th sizes only

Work 1 round in MS, decreasing 1 st at centre of front, back, and each sleeve. 144/160 sts.

**All sizes**

Joining in colours as required, work the patt from chart B, repeating the 8 patt sts 17/18/19/20/21/22 times around yoke.

**1st and 2nd sizes**

Omit rounds 10, 11, 13, 14, 20, 21, 23, 24 and 29, and decrease on rounds 12, 22, 27, and 30.

**3rd and 4th sizes**

Omit rounds 10, 13, 14, 20, 23, 24, and 29, and decrease on rounds 12, 22, 27, and 30.

**5th and 6th sizes**

Work all 32 rounds and decrease on rounds 12, 22, 27, and 30.

**All sizes**

Break off 2nd C, and with 1st C decrease in next round as follows: (k2, k2 tog) to end of round. 51/54/57/60/63/66 sts.

**Next Round**

**1st, 3rd and 5th sizes** (k4, k2 tog) to the last 3 sts, k1, k2 tog. 42/47/52 sts.

**2nd, 4th and 6th sizes** (k4, k2 tog) to end of round. 45/50/55 sts.

Change to 5mm needles and work in k1, p1 rib (decrease 1 st at beg of first round on 2nd 3rd and 5th sizes) until rib measures 8/8/9/9/10/10cm (3/3/3½/3½/4/4in).
Cast off loosely and evenly.

**FINISHING**

To block and press see Guide to Techniques. Graft underarm sts together.

# Swedish Sweater

## Boy's or girl's sweater (ages 2–11)

> *Late lies the wintry sun a-bed,*
> *A frosty, fiery sleepy-head;*
> *Blinks but an hour or two; and then,*
> *A blood-red orange, sets again.*

A bright, straight-forward sweater, in the red favoured by the knitters from Dalarna in Sweden. An uncomplicated shape and simple patterns – ideal for the newcomer to the Fair Isle technique.

## SIZES

Approx age: 2–3/4–5/6–7/8–9/10–11 years
To fit chest: 56/61/66/71/76cm (22/24/26/28/30in)
Length from top of shoulder: 35/38/42.5/45/51cm (13¾/15/16¾/17¾/20in)
Sleeve seam: 28/32/35/39/43cm (11/12½/13¾/15½/17in)

## YARN

3/4/4/5/6 50g balls of DK yarn in MS
1 50g ball of same in 1st C
1/1/1/2/2 50g balls of same in 2nd C
The yarn used in this garment is Hayfield Grampian DK, in the following shades: MS – Scarlet; 1st C – Bottle; 2nd C – Cream

## NEEDLES

1 pair each 3¼mm, 4mm, and 4½mm needles

## TENSION

24 sts and 28 rows to 10cm (4in), measured over st.st. using 4mm needles.

## BACK

** With 3¼mm needles and MS, cast on 64/68/72/78/82 sts.
K1, p1 rib for 5/5/5.5/7/7cm (2/2/2¼/2¾/2¾in).

**Next row: increase**
Rib 2/4/1/4/1, (m1, rib 6/5/5/5/5) 10/12/14/14/16 times, m1, rib 2/4/1/4/1. 75/81/87/93/99 sts.
Using 4½mm needles for colour work and 4mm needles for the plain MS rows, work the patt from chart, repeating the 8 patt sts 9/10/10/11/12 times across, and working the first 1/0/3/2/1 sts and the last 2/1/4/3/2 sts on k rows, and the first 2/1/4/3/2 sts and the last 1/0/3/2/1 sts on p rows as indicated. **
Continue in this manner, repeating the 28 patt rows and working 73/82/90/94/107 rows altogether. Break off all yarns.
Place 23/25/27/29/31 sts on each side on spare needles, and place the centre 27/31/33/35/37 sts on a length of yarn for back neck.

## FRONT

As back from ** to **.
Continue in this manner, repeating the 28

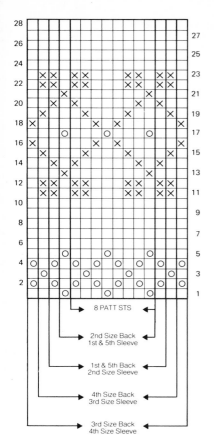

8 PATT STS

2nd Size Back
1st & 5th Sleeve

1st & 5th Back
2nd Size Sleeve

4th Size Back
3rd Size Sleeve

3rd Size Back
4th Size Sleeve

patt rows and working 63/69/77/81/93 rows altogether.

## Shape neck

Patt 28/31/33/35/38 sts. Place the rem sts on a spare needle.

Turn, and keeping continuity of patt, decrease 1 st at beg (neck edge) of next and every foll alt row until 23/25/27/29/31 sts remain.

**2nd, 3rd, and 4th sizes only** Patt 1 more row.

## All sizes

Place the sts on a spare needle.

Place the next (centre front) 19/19/21/23/23 sts on a length of yarn for front neck.

With wrong side facing, rejoin yarns to the rem sts and patt to end of row.

Then work as previous side, decreasing 1 st at neck edge of next and every foll alt row. Place the rem 23/25/27/29/31 sts on a length of yarn.

## SLEEVES

With 3¼mm needles and MS, cast on 34/34/36/36/38 sts.

K1, p1 rib for 5/5/5/6/6cm (2/2/2/2½/2½in).

### Next row: increase

Rib 2/1/2/3/4, (m1, rib 5/4/4/3/3) 6/8/8/10/10 times, m1, rib 2/1/2/3/4. 41/43/45/47/49 sts.

Using 4½mm needles for colour work and 4mm needles for plain MS rows, work the patt from chart, repeating the 8 patt sts 5/5/5/5/6 times across, and working the first 0/1/2/3/0 sts and the last 1/2/3/4/1 sts on k rows, and the first 1/2/3/4/1 sts and the last 0/1/2/3/0 sts on p rows as indicated.

Continue in this manner, increasing 1 st at each end of 3rd patt row, and every foll 5th row (working all increased sts into patt) until there are 63/67/73/79/83 sts.

Continue straight until 56/66/73/81/90 patt rows have been worked altogether.

Cast off all sts evenly.

## FINISHING

To block and press see Guide to Techniques.

With right sides of back and front together, join left shoulder by casting off together the 23/25/27/29/31 sts of back and front shoulder.

## Collar

With right side facing, 4mm needles and MS, pick up and knit the 27/31/33/35/37 sts of back neck, knit up 9/11/11/11/13 sts down left side of neck, pick up and knit the 19/19/21/23/23 sts of front neck, knit up 9/11/11/11/13 sts up right side of neck. 64/72/76/80/86 sts.

K1, p1 rib for 11/12/13/14/15cm (4¼/4¾/5¼/5½/6in).

Cast off loosely and evenly in rib.

With right sides together, cast off the sts of right shoulder as left.

Sew up collar seam.

Join sleeves to body, placing centre top of sleeves at shoulder seams.

Sew up side and sleeve seams.

# Swedish Pullover

### Boy's pullover (ages 6–13)

Smart schooldays. The pattern comes from a Swedish sock, which in turn was inspired by a piece of Swedish weaving.

## SIZES
Approx age: 6–7/8–9/10–11/12–13 years
To fit chest: 66/71/76/80cm (26/28/30/31½in)
Length from top of shoulder: 42/46/49/52cm (16½/18/19¼/20½in)

## YARN
3/3/3/4 50 g balls of 4-ply yarn in MS
1/1/2/2 50g balls of same in C
The yarn used in this garment is Pingouin Pingolaine in the following shades: MS – Delft; C – Marine

## NEEDLES
1 pair each 2¾mm and 3mm needles

## TENSION
17 sts and 18 rows to 5cm (2in) measured over patt, using 3mm needles.

## BACK
** With 2¾mm needles and MS, cast on 100/108/114/120 sts.
K1, p1 rib for 5/5/6/6cm (2/2/2½/2½in).

### Next row: increase
Rib 5/4/4/5, (m1, rib 5) to the last 5/4/5/5 sts; m1, rib 5/4/5/5. 119/129/135/143 sts.
Change to 3mm needles and joining in C, work the patt from chart, repeating the 5 patt sts

23/25/26/28 times across, and working the first 2/2/2/1 sts and the last 2/2/3/2 sts on k rows, and the first 2/2/3/2 sts and the last 2/2/2/1 sts on p rows as indicated.
Continue in this manner until back measures 26/29/30.5/32.5cm (10¼/11¼/12/12¾in) from beg, with right side facing for next row. **

### Shape armholes
Keeping continuity of patt, cast off 5/5/6/6 sts at beg of next 2 rows.
Decrease 1 st at each end of the next 4/5/5/6 rows.
Patt 1 row straight, then decrease 1 st at each end of next and every foll alt row until 87/93/95/99 sts remain.
Continue straight in patt until armhole measures 16/17/18.5/19.5cm (6¼/6¾/7¼/7¾in), with right side facing for next row.

### Shape shoulders
Keeping continuity of patt, cast off 7/7/7/8 sts at beg of next 2 rows.
Cast off 7/8/8/8 sts at beg of next 4 rows.
Place the rem sts on a spare needle for back neck.

## FRONT
As back from ** to **.

### Shape left armhole/neck
Cast off 5/5/6/6 sts, patt the next 54/59/61/65 sts, place the rem sts on a spare needle.
Turn, and shape armhole/neck as follows:

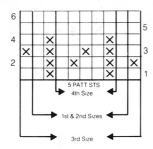

5 PATT STS
4th Size

1st & 2nd Sizes

3rd Size

Decrease 1 st at neck edge of first and every foll alt row 10 times, then decrease 1 st at neck edge of every foll 3rd row. *At the same time*, decrease 1 st at armhole edge of the first 4/5/5/6 rows, then decrease 1 st at armhole edge of every foll alt row 7/8/9/10 times. Then continue to decrease at neck edge of every 3rd row until 21/23/23/24 sts remain.

Continue straight in patt until armhole corresponds in length with back at shoulder, with right side facing for next row.

### Shape shoulder

Cast off 7/7/7/8 sts, patt to end of row.
Patt 1 row straight.
Cast off 7/8/8/8 sts, patt to end of row.
Patt 1 row straight, then cast off the rem 7/8/8/8 sts.

### Shape right armhole/neck

With right side facing, place the centre st on a safety pin, then rejoin yarn to the sts on spare needle and patt to end of row.
Shape armhole/neck as left side, in reverse.

### FINISHING

To block and press see Guide to Techniques.
Sew up right shoulder seam.

### Neck border

With right side facing, 2¾mm needles and MS, knit up 50/54/58/62 sts down left side of neck, knit the centre st from safety pin (mark this st with a coloured thread), knit up 51/55/59/63 sts up right side of neck, pick up and knit the 45/47/49/51 sts from back neck.
Rib as follows:
Row 1: * p1, k1; rep from * to within 2 sts of marked st, p2 tog, p1, p2tog–b, ** k1, p1; rep from ** to end of row
Row 2: k1, * p1, k1; rep from * to within 2 sts of marked st, p2 tog, k1, p2 tog–b, k1, ** p1, k1; rep from ** to end of row.
Repeat these 2 rows until border measures 2/2/2.5/2.5cm (¾/¾/1/1in).
Cast off evenly in rib, decreasing 1 st at each side of marked st as before.
Sew up left shoulder seam.

### Armhole borders

With right side facing, 2¾mm needles and MS, knit up 98/106/116/122 sts along armhole edge.
K1, p1 rib for 2/2/2.5/2.5cm (¾/¾/1/1in).
Cast off evenly in rib.
Sew up side seams.

*Colour photograph, see overleaf.*

# Norwegian Sweaters

## Boy's or girl's sweaters (ages 4–13)

> *Close by the jolly fire I sit*
> *To warm my frozen bones a bit;*
> *Or with a reindeer sled explore*
> *The colder countries round the door.*

Reindeer or dancers . . . take your pick! These casual raglan sweaters are unmistakeably
Nordic, and suitable for boys and girls of all ages.

## SIZES

Approx age: 4–5/6–7/8–9/10–11/12–13 years
To fit chest: 61/66/71/75/79cm (24/26/28/29½/
31in)
Length from back neck: 38/42/46/49/52cm
(15/16½/18/19¼/20½in)
Sleeve seam: 27/31/34/38/41cm (10½/12¼/13½/
15/16in)

## YARN

5/6/6/7/7 50g balls of Aran yarn in MS
2 50g balls of Aran yarn in C
The yarn used in both garments is EMU Aran
in the following shades:
Reindeer Sweater: MS – Fiord; C – Natural
Dancing Figures Sweater: MS – Natural; C –
Beaver

## NEEDLES

1 pair each 4mm and 5½mm needles

## TENSION

19 sts and 22 rows to 10cm (4in), measured
over chart A using 5½mm needles.

## BACK

* With 4mm needles and MS, cast on 52/56/
58/62/66 sts.
K1, p1 rib for 5/5/6/6/6cm (2/2/2½/2½/2½in).

**Next row: increase**
Rib 2/1/1/3/1, (m1, rib 8/9/7/7/8) 6/6/8/8/8
times, m1, rib 2/1/1/3/1. 59/63/67/71/75 sts.
Change to 5½mm needles and joining in C,
work the patt from chart A, repeating the 4
patt sts 14/15/16/17/18 times across, and
working the first st and the last 2 sts on k
rows, and the first 2 sts and the last st on p
rows as indicated. Continue in this manner
until back measures 12/14½/17/19½/22½cm (4¾/
5¾/6¾/7¾/8¾in) from beg, with right side facing
for next row.
Now work the 22 rows of patt from chart B (1
or 2), repeating the 18 patt sts 3/3/3/3/4 times
across, and working the first 2/4/6/8/1 sts and
the last 3/5/7/9/2 sts on k rows, and the first
3/5/7/9/2 sts and the last 2/4/6/8/1 sts on p rows
as indicated.
Now work the patt from chart A as previously
and patt 2 rows (right side should face for
next row).

*Opposite: Swedish Pullover, see page 60.*

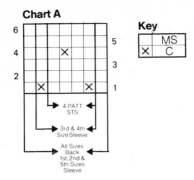

**Chart A**

Key

| | MS |
|---|---|
| ✕ | C |

4 PATT STS

3rd & 4th Size Sleeve

All Sizes Back 1st, 2nd & 5th Sizes Sleeve

## Shape armholes

Keeping continuity of patt, cast off 2/3/3/3/3 sts at beg of next 2 rows, then continue in patt and decrease for raglan as follows:
Right side rows: k1, ssk, patt to the last 3 sts, k2 tog, k1
Wrong side rows: patt straight.**
Continue in this manner until 25/25/27/29/31 sts remain. Work 1 row straight, thus right side facing for next row.

## Shape neck

k1, ssk, patt 2, k2 tog.
Turn, and patt 1 row straight. Then decrease as before, at raglan and neck edge of right side rows until 3 sts remain.
Patt 1 row straight.
Next row: sl1, k2 tog, psso and fasten off
With right side facing patt the next 11/11/13/15/17 sts and place on a holder, k2 tog, patt 2, k2 tog, k1. Turn and patt 1 row straight, then decrease as before at raglan and neck edge of right side rows until 3 sts remain.
Patt 1 row straight and finish off as previous side.

## FRONT

As back from * to **.
Continue in this manner until 27/27/31/33/35 sts remain. Work 1 row straight, thus right side facing for next row.

## Shape neck

k1, ssk, patt 4/4/6/6/6, k2 tog.
Turn, and patt 1 row straight. Then decrease as before, at raglan and neck edges of right

side rows until 3 sts remain.
Patt 1 row straight.
Next row: sl1, k2 tog, psso and fasten off.
With right side facing, rejoin yarns and patt the next 9/9/9/11/13 sts and place on a holder (front neck), k2 tog, patt 4/4/6/6/6, k2 tog, k1.
Turn and decrease as before at raglan and neck edges of right side rows until 3 sts remain.
Patt 1 row straight and finish off as previous side.

## SLEEVES

With 4 mm needles and MS, cast on 34/36/38/42/44 sts.
K1, p1, for 5/5/6/6/6cm (2/2/2½/2½/2½ins).

## Next row: increase

Rib 1/3/4/1/2, (m1, rib 4/3/3/4/4) 8/10/10/10/10 times, m1, rib 1/3/4/1/2. 43/47/49/53/55 sts
Change to 5½mm needles and joining in C, work the patt from chart A, repeating the 4 patt sts 10/11/12/13/13 times across, and working the first 1/1/0/0/1 sts and the last 2/2/1/1/2 sts on k rows, and the first 2/2/1/1/2 sts and the last 1/1/0/0/1 sts on p rows as indicated.
Continue in this manner until sleeve measures 16/20/23/27/30cm (6¼/8/9¼/10¾/11¾in) from beg with right side facing for next row.
Work the patt from chart B repeating the 18 patt sts 1/1/1/1/2 times across, and working the first 3/5/6/8/0 sts and the last 4/6/7/9/1 sts on k rows, and the first 4/6/7/9/1 sts and the last 3/5/6/8/0 sts on p rows as indicated.

## Shape top

Keeping continuity of patt, cast off 2/3/3/3/3 sts at beg of next 2 rows.
Then continue in patt and decrease for raglan as back and front, until 5/5/5/7/7 sts remain.
Patt 1 row straight, then place all sts on a holder.

## FINISHING

To block and press, see Guide to Techniques.
Join back, sleeves and front at raglan seams, leaving back/left sleeve raglan seam open.

64

## Neck

With right side facing, 4mm needles and MS, pick up and knit the 5/5/5/7/7 sts of left sleeve, knit up 7/7/9/9/9 sts down left front neck, pick up and knit the 9/9/9/11/13 sts of front neck, knit up 7/7/9/9/9 sts up right front neck, pick up and knit the 5/5/5/7/7 sts of right sleeve, knit up 5 sts down right back neck, pick up and knit the 11/11/13/15/17 sts of back neck, and knit up 5 sts up left back neck. 54/54/60/68/72 sts.

K1, p1 rib for 5/5/6/6/6cm (2/2/2½/2½/2½in). Cast off loosely and evenly.

Sew up remaining raglan seam. Fold neck rib in half to the inside and catchstitch neatly in position. Sew up side and sleeve seams.

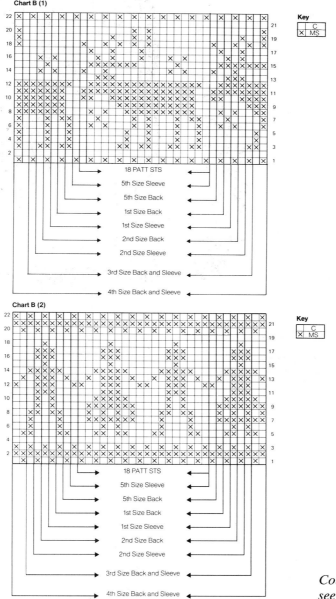

*Colour photograph, see overleaf.*

# Norwegian All-in-One Suit

### Boy's or girl's suit (ages 1–3)

Guaranteed to keep a small boy or girl warm through the winter. The pattern comes from a Norwegian sock.

**SIZES**
Approx age: 1–2/2–3 years
To fit chest: 54/56cm (21/22in)
Neck to crotch: 41/46cm (16/18in)
Inside leg seam: 30/35cm (11¾/13¾in)
Sleeve seam: 22/24cm (8½/9½in)

**YARN**
5/6 50g balls of Aran yarn in MS
4/5 50g balls of Aran yarn in C
The yarn used in this garment is Emu Aran in the following shades:
MS – Peony; C – Natural

**NEEDLES**
1 pair each 4mm and 5½mm needles

**NOTIONS**
30cm (12in) zip fastener

**TENSION**
20 sts and 20 rows to 10cm (4in) measured over chart A patt using 5½mm needles.

**RIGHT LEG**
With 4mm needles and MS, cast on 48/50 sts.
K1, p1 rib for 5cm (2in).

**Next row: increase**
Rib 2/1, (m1, rib 4) 11/12 times, m1, rib 2/1.
60/63 sts.
Change to 5½mm needles, and joining in C work the patt from chart A, repeating the 27 patt sts twice across, and working the last 6/9 sts on k rows and the first 6/9 sts on p rows as indicated.
Continue in this manner until leg measures 19/24cm (7½/9½in) from beg, with right side facing for next row.

**Shape leg**
Continue in patt and increase 1 st at each end of row and every foll 3rd row, 6 times (72/75 sts), working the increased sts in MS.
Then continue straight until leg measures 30/35cm (11¾/13¾in) from beg, with right side facing for next row.

**Shape crotch**
Continue in patt and cast off 3 sts at beg of next 2 rows.
Then decrease 1 st at each end of next and every foll alt row until 60/63 sts remain.
Patt 1 row straight (right side should now face for next row). Place these sts on a holder.

**LEFT LEG**
As right leg, but reverse the patt as indicated on chart A, repeating the 27 patt sts twice across, and working the first 5/8 sts and the

*Opposite: Norwegian Sweater, see page 63.*

## Chart A 1st Size

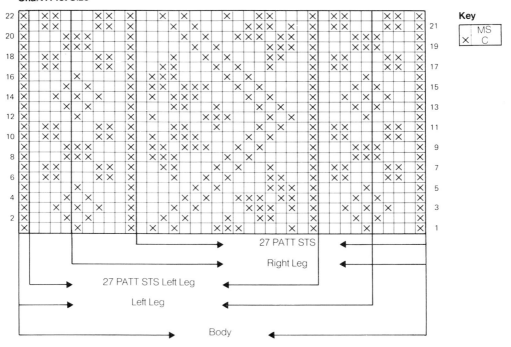

**Key**

| | MS |
|---|---|
| ✕ | C |

27 PATT STS

Right Leg

27 PATT STS Left Leg

Left Leg

Body

## Chart A 2nd Size

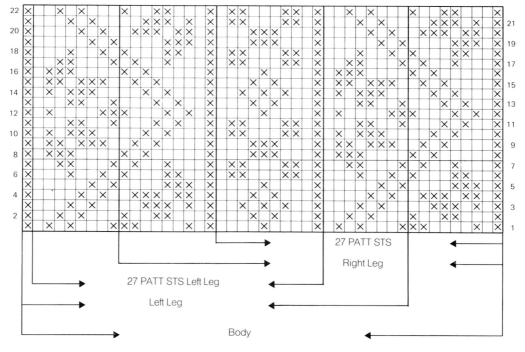

27 PATT STS

Right Leg

27 PATT STS Left Leg

Left Leg

Body

last st on k rows, and the first st and the last 5/8 sts on p rows as indicated.

Continue in this manner, shaping leg and crotch as right leg and ending on the *same* patt row.

## Join legs

With right sides of both legs facing, and working the sts of right leg first, patt across all sts (NB for 1st size k tog the last st of right leg and the first st of left leg). 119/126 sts.

Work straight in patt, i.e. repeating the 27 patt sts 4 times across, and working the last 11/18 sts on k rows and the first 11/18 sts on p rows as indicated on chart A.

Continue in this manner until body measures 29/32½cm (11¼/12¾in) from crotch cast off, with right side facing for next row.

## Right front yoke

With C, knit 28/30 sts. Place the rem sts on a spare needle.

Turn, and work yoke patt as follows:

Row 1: (wrong side) With C, p1; with MS, p1; rep to end of row

Row 2: With C, k1; with MS, k1; rep to end of row

Repeat these 2 rows, and continue straight until yoke measures 11½/12½cm (4½/5in) from beg of yoke patt, with wrong side facing for next row.

## Shape neck

Patt 21/22 sts. Place the rem 7/8 sts on a length of yarn (front neck).

Next row: K2 tog, patt to end of row.

## Shape Shoulder

Cast off 5 sts at beg of next and foll alt row.

*At the same time*, decrease 1 st at neck edge of every row.

Next row: K2 tog, patt to end of row.

Cast off the rem 6/7 sts.

## Back Yoke

With right side facing, and C, cast off the next 3 sts then knit the next 57/60 sts from spare needle.

Turn, and patt as follows:

### 1st size

Row 1: (wrong side) with C, p1; with MS, p1; rep to last st, then with C, p1

Row 2: With MS, k1; with C, k1; rep to the last st, then with MS, k1

### 2nd size

Patt as front yoke.

### Both sizes

Continue in this manner until back yoke corresponds in length with front yoke, with right side facing for next row.

## Shape shoulders

Keeping continuity of patt, cast off 5 sts at beg of next 4 rows.

Then cast off 6/7 sts at beg of next 2 rows.

Place the rem 25/26 sts on a holder (back neck).

## Left front yoke

With right side facing, and C, cast off the next 3 sts, knit the rem 28/30 sts from spare needle.

Work left yoke as right but reversing all shapings.

## SLEEVES

With 4mm needles and MS, cast on 34/36 sts. K1, p1 rib for 4cm (1½in).

### Next row: increase

First size: k1, (m1, k2) 16 times, m1, k1. (51 sts)

Second size: k1, (m1, k1) 3 times, (m1, k2) 14 times, (m1, k1) 4 times. (57 sts)

Change to 5½mm needles, and joining in C work the patt from chart B, repeating the 20 patt sts twice across, and working the first 5/8 sts and the last 6/9 sts on k rows, and the first 6/9 sts and the last 5/8 sts on p rows as indicated.

Continue in this manner until sleeve measures 22/24cm (8½/9½in) from beg, with wrong side facing for next row.

**Chart B**

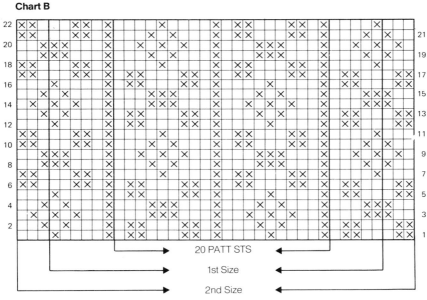

**Key** As Chart A

Break off MS, and with C purl 1 row. Then with C cast off all sts.

## FINISHING

To block and press see Guide to Techniques

Join inside leg seams.

Join crotch seam, beginning at back and stitching around front, leaving the front opening to measure 30cm (12in) from neck.

Join shoulder seams.

Sew up sleeve seams from cuffs to within $\frac{1}{2}$cm ($\frac{1}{4}$in) of top.

Insert sleeves, stitching cast off edges of sleeves to armhole, and stitching $\frac{1}{2}$cm ($\frac{1}{4}$in) ends of sleeve seams to cast off sts underarms.

### Collar

With 4mm needles, MS, and right side facing, pick up and k the 7/8 sts from right front neck, knit up 7 sts up right side of neck, pick up and k the 25/26 sts of back neck, knit up 7 sts down left side of neck, and pick up and k the 7/8 sts of left front neck. 53/56 sts.

K1, p1 rib (first size having a k1 at each end of first and alt rows) for 4 rows.

Change to 5$\frac{1}{2}$mm needles and rib for a further 5cm (2in).

Cast off loosely and evenly.

### Right front rib

With 4mm needles, MS, and right side facing, knit up 50 sts along right front opening.

K1, p1 rib for 4 rows.

Cast off loosely and evenly.

Insert zip fastener so that rib overlaps to conceal.

# Faroe

## Girl's coat, hat and legwarmers (ages 4–9)

> *Black are my steps on silver sod;*
> *Thick blows my frosty breath abroad;*
> *And tree and house, and hill and lake,*
> *Are frosted like a wedding cake.*

Simple and effective geometry from the Faroe Islands.

## SIZES
Approx age: 4–5/6–7/8–9 years
To fit chest: 61/66/71cm (24/26/28in)
Length from top of shoulder: 57/62/67cm
(22½/24½/26½in)
Sleeve seam: 27/31/34cm (10½/12¼/13½in)

## YARN
11/12/14 50g balls of chunky yarn in MS
2/3/3 50g balls of same in 1st C
50g ball of same in each of 2nd, 3rd, 4th, and
5th C
The yarn used in this garment is Hayfield
Gaucho in the following shades:
MS – Llama; 1st C – Rio; 2nd C – Inca; 3rd C
– Chico; 4th C – Tequila; 5th C – Caramba

## NEEDLES
1 pair each 5mm and 6½mm needles
1 set of 4 or circular 5mm and 6½mm needles
for hat and legwarmers

## NOTIONS
8/8/9 buttons

## TENSION
15 sts and 17 rows to 10cm (4in), measured
over chart A patt using 6½mm needles.

## COAT

### BACK
With 5mm needles and MS, cast on 46/50/54
sts.
K1, p1 rib for 3/3/4cm (1¼/1¼/1½in).

**Next row: increase**
Rib 1, (m1, rib 11/12/13) 4 times, m1, rib 1.
(51/55/59 sts)
Change to 6½mm needles, and joining in 1st
C, work the patt from chart A, repeating the
4 patt sts 12/13/14 times across, and working
the first st and the last 2 sts on k rows, and the
first 2 sts and the last st on p rows as
indicated. Work rows 1 to 3 once only, and
thereafter repeat rows 4 to 9 until back
measures 41/45/49cm (16¼/17¾/19¼in) from
beg, with right side facing for next row.
With MS and 1st C, work the first 3 rows of
patt from chart B, repeating the 6 patt sts

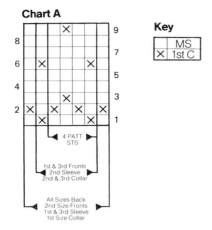

**Chart A**

**Key**

| | MS |
|---|---|
| X | 1st C |

4 PATT STS

1st & 3rd Fronts
2nd Sleeve
2nd & 3rd Collar

All Sizes Back
2nd Size Fronts
1st & 3rd Sleeve
1st Size Collar

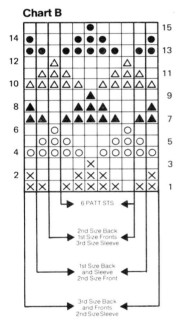

**Chart B**

**Key**

| | MS |
|---|---|
| X | 1st C |
| O | 2nd C |
| ▲ | 3rd C |
| △ | 4th C |
| ● | 5th C |

6 PATT STS

2nd Size Back
1st Size Fronts
3rd Size Sleeve

1st Size Back
and Sleeve
2nd Size Front

3rd Size Back
and Fronts
2nd Size Sleeve

8/9/9 times across and working the first 1/0/2 sts and the last 2/1/3 sts on k rows, and the first 2/1/3 sts and the last 1/0/2 sts on p rows as indicated.

Now with wrong side facing, shape armholes as follows:

Keeping continuity of chart B, and joining in colours as required, cast off 2/3/3 sts at beg of next 2 rows.

Decrease 1 st at each end of next row.

Patt 1 row straight, then decrease 1 st at each end of next and every foll alt row until 41/43/45 sts remain.

Continue straight in patt until back measures 57/62/67cm (22½/24½/26½in), with right side facing for next row.

### Shape shoulders

Keeping continuity of patt, cast off 4 sts at beg of next 4 rows.

Cast off 4/5/5 sts at beg of next 2 rows.

Place the rem 15/17/19 sts on a holder for back neck.

### RIGHT FRONT

With 5mm needles and MS, cast on 22/24/26 sts.

K1, p1 rib for 3/3/4cm (1¼/1¼/1½in).

### Next row: increase

Rib 4, m1, (rib 7/8/9, m1) twice, rib 4 (25/27/29 sts)

Change to 6½mm needles, and joining in 1st C, work the patt from chart A, repeating the 4 patt sts 6/6/7 times across, and working the first 0/1/0 sts and the last 1/2/1 sts on k rows, and the first 1/2/1 sts and the last 0/1/0 sts on p rows as indicated. Work rows 1 to 3 once only, and thereafter repeat rows 4 to 9 until front corresponds in length with back at end of chart A patt, with right side facing for next row.

With MS and 1st C, work the first 3 rows of chart B, repeating the 6 patt sts 4 times across, and working the first 0/1/2 sts and the last 1/2/3 sts on k rows, and the first 1/2/3 sts and the last 0/1/2 sts on p rows as indicated.

Now with wrong side facing, shape armhole as follows:

Keeping continuity of patt, and joining in colours as required, cast off 2/3/3 sts at beg of next row.

Decrease 1 st at end of next row.

Patt 1 row straight, then decrease 1 st at armhole edge of next and every foll alt row until 20/21/22 sts remain.

Continue straight in patt until front measures 55/60/65cm (22/24/26in) from beg, with wrong side facing for next row.

**Shape neck**

Patt to the last 4/4/5 sts. Place these sts on a safety pin for front neck. Keeping continuity of patt, decrease 1 st at neck edge of next 3 rows, then decrease 1 st at neck edge of next alt row. *At the same time*, when front corresponds in length with back at shoulder, with wrong side facing, shape shoulder as follows:

Cast off 4 sts at beg of next and foll alt row. Patt 1 row straight, then cast off the rem 4/5/5 sts.

## LEFT FRONT

As right front but reversing all shapings, and working armhole cast off on 3rd row of chart B.

## SLEEVES

With 5mm needles and MS, cast on 20/22/22 sts.

K1, p1 rib for 4/5/5cm (1½/2/2in).

**Next row: increase**

K 1/3/1, (m1, k1) to end of row. (39/41/43 sts) Change to 6½mm needles and joining in 1st C, work the patt from chart A, repeating the 4 patt sts 9/10/10 times across, and working the first 1/0/1 sts and the last 2/1/2 sts on k rows, and the first 2/1/2 sts and the last 1/0/1 sts on p rows as indicated. Work rows 1 to 3 once only, and thereafter repeat rows 4 to 9 until sleeve measures 25/29/32 cm (10/11½/12¾in) from beg, with right side facing for next row. With MS and 1st C, work the first 3 rows of chart B, repeating the 6 patt sts 6/6/7 times across, and working the first 1/2/0 sts and the last 2/3/1 sts on k rows, and the first 2/3/1 sts and the last 1/2/0 sts on p rows as indicated. Now with wrong side facing, shape top as follows:

Keeping continuity of chart B, and joining in colours as required, cast off 2/3/3 sts at beg of next 2 rows.

Decrease 1 st at each end of next row.

Patt 1/3/3 rows straight, then decrease 1 st at each end of next and every foll alt row until 25 sts remain.

Decrease 1 st at each end of every row until 11/13/13 sts remain.

Cast off 3 sts at beg of next 2 rows. Cast off the rem 5/7/7 sts.

## FINISHING

To block and press see Guide to Techniques. Join fronts to back at shoulders.

**Collar**

With 5mm needles, MS and right side facing, pick up and k the 4/4/5 sts of right front neck, knit up 6 sts up right side of neck, pick up and k the 15/17/19 sts of back neck, knit up 6 sts down left side of neck, and pick up and k the 4/4/5 sts of left front neck. (35/37/41 sts) Change to 6½mm needles and p 1 row.

Join in 1st C and patt the first 5 rows of patt from chart A, repeating the 4 patt sts 8/9/10 times across, and working the first 1/0/0 sts and the last 2/1/1 sts on k rows, and the first 2/1/1 sts and the last 1/0/0 sts on p rows as indicated.

Now work 5 rows in k1, p1 rib (first and alt rows having a k st at each end).

Cast off loosely and evenly.

Fold collar in half to the inside and catchstitch neatly in position.

Sew up side and sleeve seams. Insert sleeves, gathering any fullness at the top.

**Button band**

With 5mm needles and MS, cast on 6 sts.

K1, p1 rib until band, when slightly stretched, fits along left front to top of collar. Sew up as you go along.

**Buttonhole band**

Work as button band with the addition of 8/8/9 buttonholes, first to come 2½cm (1in) from bottom, and last to come 1cm (½in) from top, the remainder spaced evenly between. Sew up as you go along.

Sew on buttons to correspond with buttonholes.

## HAT

With set or circular 5mm needles, cast on 68/72/76 sts.
K1, p1 rib for 10cm (4in).

**Next round: increase**
Rib 4/0/4, (m1, rib 8) 8/9/9 times. (76/80/84 sts)
Change to 6½mm needles and work the patt from chart A, repeating the 4 patt sts 19/20/21 times around, and working the first 3 rounds of chart once only, and thereafter repeating rounds 4 to 9 until hat measures 17/19/20cm (6¾/7½/8in) from beg of chart patt. Break off 1st C.

**Next round: decrease**
K2 tog to end of round.
K 1 round, then decrease as previous decrease round.
Break off MS, leaving a length long enough to pass through the remaining sts and fasten off.

## LEGWARMERS

With set or circular 5mm needles, cast on 28/32/34 sts.
K1, p1 rib for 4cm (1½in).

**Next round: increase**
Rib 0/0/4, (m1, rib 7/8/5) 4/4/6 times. (32/36/40 sts)
Change to 6½mm needles and joining in 1st C, work the patt from chart A, repeating the 4 patt sts 8/9/10 times, and working rounds 1 to 3 once only, and thereafter repeating rounds 4 to 9 until piece measures 18/19/20cm (7/7½/8in) from beg.
Work rounds 1 to 4 once more.
Change to 5mm needles and k1, p1 rib for 8cm (3in).
Cast off loosely and evenly.

# Finland

## Girl's dress and cardigan (ages 6–11)

A cardigan and dress using similar glove patterns to very different effects. Festive, and with the Eastern flavour so typical of many Finnish gloves and mittens.

## CARDIGAN

### SIZES
Approx age: 6–7/8–9/10–11 years
To fit chest 66/71/76cm (26/28/30in)
Length from top of shoulder: 42/46/49cm (16½/18/19¼in)
Sleeve seam: 35/39/43cm (13¾/15¼/17in)

### YARN
2/3/3 50g balls of mohair mix DK yarn in MS
1/2/2 50g balls of same in each of 1st C and 2nd C
1/1/2 50g balls of same in 3rd C
1 50g ball of same in 4th C
The yarn used in this garment is Emu Mistique in the following shades:
MS – Clover; 1st C – Greengage; 2nd C – Grape; 3rd C – Lemon Mousse; 4th C – Windsor

### NEEDLES
1 pair each 3¾mm and 4½mm needles

### NOTIONS
10 buttons

### TENSION
27 sts and 28 rows to 10cm (4in), measured over patt using 4½mm needles.

### BACK
With 3¾mm needles and MS, cast on 86/94/102 sts.
K1, p1, rib for 6cm (2½in).

**Next row: increase**
Rib 1/1/2, (m1, rib 7) 12/13/14 times, m1, rib 1/2/2. (99/108/117 sts)
Change to 4½mm needles and work patt as follows:
Row 1: (right side) * m1 (by knitting into front and back of st), k2, sl1 – k2 tog – psso, k2, m1; rep from * to end of row
Row 2: Purl
Row 3: As row 1
Row 4: Knit.
Repeat rows 1 to 4, changing colours every 4 rows as follows:
4 rows MS; 4 rows 1st C; 4 rows 2nd C; 4 rows 3rd C.
Continue in this manner until back measures 26/29/31cm (10¼/11¼/12¼in) from beg, with right side facing for next row.

**Shape armholes**
Change to 4th C, cast off the first 5 sts, k to end of row.
Next row: Cast off the first 5 sts, p to end of row.
Break off 4th C, and joining in colours as required, work the patt from chart A, repeating the 26 patt sts 3/3/4 times across, and working the first 5/10/1 sts and the last 6/10/2 sts on k rows, and the first 6/10/2 sts

**Chart A**

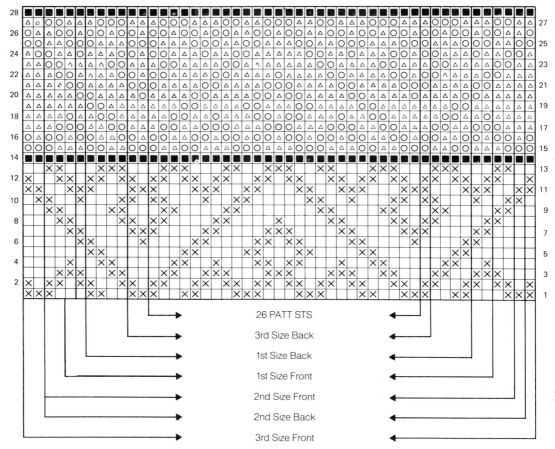

26 PATT STS
3rd Size Back
1st Size Back
1st Size Front
2nd Size Front
2nd Size Back
3rd Size Front

and the last 5/10/1 sts on p rows as indicated.
Continue in this manner until all 28 rows of
chart A have been worked.
Then work the patt from chart B, and
continue until armhole measures 16/17/18cm
(6¼/6¾/7in) from cast off sts, with right side
facing for next row.

### Shape shoulders
Keeping cont. of patt, cast off 7/8/9 sts at beg
of next 8 rows.
Leave the rem 33/34/35 sts on a holder (back
neck).

### RIGHT FRONT
With 3¾mm needles and MS, cast on 41/45/49
sts.

K1, p1, rib (right side rows ending with a k1)
for 6cm (2½in).

### Next row: increase
Rib 1/0/0, (m1, rib 13/11/12) 3/4/4 times, m1,
rib 1. 45/50/54 sts.
Change to 4½mm needles.

### 1st and 3rd sizes
Patt and change colours as back.

### 2nd size
Changing colours as back, patt as follows:
Row 1: (right side) k2 tog, k2, m1, * m1, k2,
    sl1 – k2 tog – psso, k2, m1; rep from * to
    end of row
Row 2: Purl
Row 3: As row 1

80

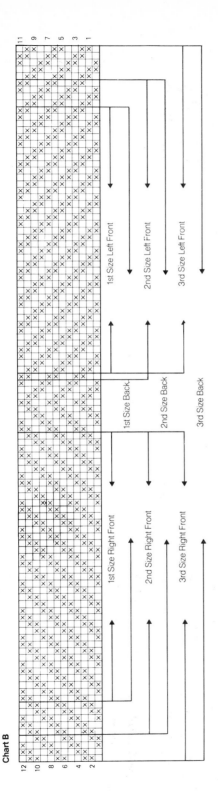

Chart B

Row 4: Knit.
Repeat rows 1 to 4.

**All sizes**
Continue in patt until front corresponds in
length with back, with right side facing for
next row.
Change to 4th C and knit 1 row.

**Shape armhole**
With 4th C, cast off the first 5 sts, purl to end
of row.
Break off 4th C and joining in colours as
required, work the patt from chart A,
working the 26 patt sts once, and working the
first 7/9/11 sts and the last 7/10/12 sts on k
rows, and the first 7/10/12 sts and the last
7/9/11 sts on p rows as indicated.
Continue in this manner until all 28 rows of
chart A have been worked. Then work the
right front patt from chart B, and continue
straight until front measures 14/15/16cm (5½/
5¾/6¼in) from cast off sts, with wrong side
facing for next row.

**Shape neck**
Patt to the last 5/6/6 sts, place these sts on a
length of yarn.
Turn, and keeping cont. of patt, decrease 1 st
at neck edge of next 4 rows.
Then decrease 1 st at neck edge of every foll
alt row 3 times. *At the same time*, when front
corresponds in length with back at shoulder
edge, with wrong side facing, shape shoulder
as follows:
Keeping cont. of patt, cast off 7/8/9 sts at beg
of next and foll alt rows, 4 times.

**LEFT FRONT**
As right front, reversing shapings and
working left front patt from chart B.

**NB: 2nd size only**
Read row 1 of main patt as follows:
*m1, k2, sl1 – k2 tog – psso, k2, m1; rep from
* to the last 4 sts, m1, k2, k2 tog.

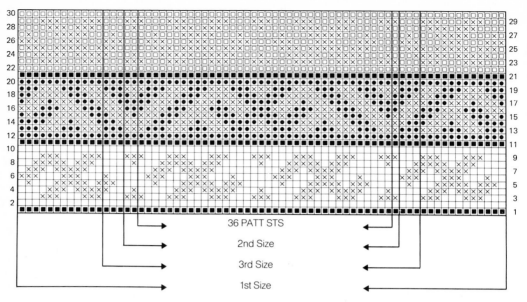

**Key**

| | |
|---|---|
| ■ | MS |
| | 1st C |
| ✕ | 2nd C |
| ● | 3rd C |
| □ | 4th C |

## SLEEVES

With 3¾mm needles and MS, cast on 48/50/52 sts.
K1, p1, rib for 6cm (2½in).

**Next row: increase**
Rib 5/5/4, k twice into every st to the last 5 sts, rib 5. 86/90/95 sts.
Change to 4½mm needles

**1st and 3rd sizes**
Changing colours as back, patt as for 2nd size front.

**2nd size**
Change colours and patt as back.

**All sizes**
Continue straight until sleeve measures 37/41/45cm (14½/16/17¾in) from beg, with right side facing for next row.
Break off all colours and joining in 4th C, work 2 rows st.st.
Cast off all sts.

## FINISHING

To block and press see Guide to Techniques. Join fronts to back at shoulder seams. Insert sleeves.
Sew up side and sleeve seams.

**Neck**
With 3¾mm needles, 4th C, and right side facing, knit the 5/6/6 sts from right front neck, knit up 10 sts up right side, pick up and knit the 33/34/35 sts of back neck, knit up 10 sts down left side and knit the 5/6/6 sts from left front neck. 63/66/67 sts.
Work 6 rows in garter st. (k every row)
Cast off evenly.

**Left front opening**
With 3¾mm needles and 4th C, and right side facing, knit up 97/106/115 sts along opening.
Work 6 rows in garter st.
Cast off evenly.

**Right front opening**
As left front opening, but work 3 rows garter st.

**Next row: make buttonholes**
K3, (yo, k2 tog, k 8/9/10) 9 times, yo, k2 tog, k2.
K 2 more rows.
Cast off evenly.
Sew on buttons to correspond with buttonholes.


## *DRESS*


### SIZES
Approx age: 2–3/4–5/6–7 years
To fit chest: 56/61/66cm (22/24/26in)
Length from top of shoulder: 47/56/64cm (18½/22/25in)
Sleeve seam: 28/32/36cm (11/12½/14¼in)


### YARN
6/7/8 50g balls of DK yarn in MS
1 50g ball in each of 1st, 2nd, 3rd and 4th C
The yarn used in this garment is Emu Superwash DK in the following shades:
MS – Regency; 1st C – Geranium; 2nd C – Claret Cup; 3rd C – Smokey Pink; 4th C – Natural.


### NEEDLES
1 pair each 4mm and 3¼mm needles
3.50mm crochet hook


### TENSION
12 sts and 13 rows to 5cm (2in) measured over chart patt using 4mm needles.


### BACK
** With 4mm needles and MS, cast on 106/119/132 sts.
Knit 4 rows.

Patt as follows:
Row 1: (right side) k1, ssk, k4, yo, * k1, yo, k4, k2 tog, ssk, k4, yo; rep from * to the last 8 sts; k1, yo, k4, k2 tog, k1
Row 2: Purl
Row 3: As Row 1
Row 4: As Row 2
Row 5: As Row 1
Row 6: As Row 2
Row 7: Purl
Row 8: Knit.
Repeat these 8 rows 4/5/6 times more. (40/48/56 patt rows altogether)

**Next row: work 1st decrease (row 1 of patt)**
k1, ssk, k2, k2 tog, yo, * k1, yo, ssk, k2, k2 tog, ssk, k2, k2 tog, yo; rep from * to the last 8 sts; k1, yo, ssk, k2, k2 tog, k1. 90/103/112 sts. Work the rem patt rows as before, but having 1 st less at each side of chevrons.
Continue straight in patt until the 8 patt rows have been worked 7/9/10 times from beg.

**Next row: work 2nd decrease (row 1 of patt)**
k1, ssk, k1, k2 tog, * k1, yo, ssk, k1, k2 tog, ssk, k1, k2 tog, yo; rep from * to the last 7 sts; k1, yo, ssk, k1, k2 tog, k1. 74/85/92 sts.
Work the rem patt rows as before, working 1 st less at each side of chevrons.
Continue straight until the 8 patt rows have been worked 9/11/13 times from beg.

**Next row: decrease for waist**
k 0/1/0, * k2 tog, k 16/7/7; rep from * to the last 2/3/2 sts; k2 tog, k 0/1/0. 69/75/81 sts.
Purl 1 row.
Change to 3¼mm needles and k1, p1 rib for 4/4/6 rows (right side rows having a k st at each end).

**Next row: make eyelets**
Rib 1/3/1, * yo, k2 tog, p1, k1; rep from * to end of row.
Rib for a further 3/3/5 rows.
Change to 4mm needles and joining in and breaking off colours as required, work the patt from chart, repeating the 36 patt sts once/twice/twice across, and working the first 16/1/4 sts and the last 17/2/5 sts on k rows, and

83

the first 17/2/5 sts and the last 16/1/4 sts on p
rows as indicated.
Continue in this manner until back measures
10/11/13cm (4/4½/5in) from beg of chart patt,
with right side facing for next row.

### Shape armholes

Keeping continuity of patt, cast off 3 sts at
beg of next 2 rows.
Decrease 1 st at each end of next 3 rows.
Patt 1 row straight, then decrease 1 st at each
end of next and every foll alt row until 53/57/
61 sts remain. **
Continue straight in patt until back measures
21/24/27cm (8¼/9½/10½in) from beg of chart
patt, with right side facing for next row.

### Shape shoulders

Keeping continuity of patt, cast off 5 sts at
beg of next 2 rows.
Cast off 5/5/6 sts at beg of next 2 rows
Cast off 5/6/6 sts at beg of next 2 rows
Cast off the rem 23/25/27 sts for back neck.


### FRONT

As back from ** to **. Patt 1 row straight.

### Divide for front opening

With right side facing, patt 26/28/30 sts. Place
the rem sts on a spare needle.
Turn and keeping continuity of patt, work
these 26/28/30 sts until left front measures
19/21/23cm (7½/8¼/9in) from beg of chart patt,
with wrong side facing for next row.

### Left neck/shoulder

Keeping continuity of patt, cast off 7/7/8 sts,
patt to end of row.
Decrease 1 st at end (neck edge) of next and
every foll alt row 4/5/5 times. *At the same
time*, when front corresponds in length with
back at armhole, with right side facing for
next row, cast off for shoulder as follows:
Keeping continuity of patt, cast off 5 sts, patt
to end of row.
Patt 1 row straight. Cast off 5/5/6 sts, patt to
end of row.

Patt 1 row straight, then cast off the rem 5/6/6
sts.

### Right side/neck/shoulder

With right side facing, rejoin yarn and cast off
the first st (centre front), patt the rem 26/28/
30 sts.
Turn and work as left side/neck/shoulder,
reversing all shapings.

### SLEEVES

With 4mm needles and MS, cast on 68/72/79
sts.
Knit 4 rows.
Patt as follows:
Row 1: (right side) k 1/3/1, ssk, k3, yo, * k1,
    yo, k3, k2 tog, ssk, k3, yo; rep from * to the
    last 7/9/7 sts; k1, yo, k3, k2 tog, k 1/3/1
Row 2: Purl.
Repeat these 2 rows once more.

### Next row: decrease

k 1/3/1, ssk, k1, k2 tog, yo, * k1, yo, ssk, k1,
k2 tog, ssk, k1, k2 tog, yo; rep from * to the
last 7/9/7 sts; k1, yo, ssk, k1, k2 tog, k 1/3/1.
56/60/65 sts.
Purl 1 row.
Change to 3¼mm needles and k1, p1 rib (3rd
size having a k st at each end of right side
row) for 2 rows.

### Next row: make eyelets

* k1, p1, yo, k2 tog; rep from * to the last
0/0/1 st; k 0/0/1. k1, p1 rib for a further 3
rows.
Change to 4mm needles and patt as follows:
Row 1: (right side) k 1/3/1, ssk, k2, yo, * k1,
    yo, k2, k2 tog, ssk, k2, yo; rep from * to the
    last 6/8/6 sts; k1, yo, k2, k2 tog, k 1/3/1
Row 2: Purl
Row 3: As Row 1
Row 4: As Row 2
Row 5: As Row 1
Row 6: As Row 2
Row 7: Purl
Row 8: Knit.
Repeat rows 1 to 8 until sleeve measures 28/
32/36cm (11/12½/14¼in) from beg (measuring

from longest point of chevron), with right side facing for next row.

## Shape top
Keeping continuity of patt as far as possible, cast off 3 sts at beg of next 2 rows.
Patt 2/6/6 rows straight. NB For first and 3rd sizes, begin patt row with k2, then work from *. For 2nd size begin patt row with ssk, k2, yo, then work from *.
Then decrease 1 st at each end of next and every foll alt row until 26/30/33 sts remain.
Patt 1 row straight, then decrease 1 st at each end of next and every foll row until 10/10/11 sts remain. Cast off all sts.

## COLLAR
With 4mm needles and MS, cast on 79/79/90 sts.
Knit 4 rows.
Patt as follows:
Row 1: (right side) k1, ssk, k3, yo, * k1, yo, k3, k2 tog, ssk, k3, yo; rep from * to the last 7 sts; k1, yo, k3, k2 tog, k1
Row 2: Purl
Row 3: As Row 1
Row 4: As Row 2
Row 5: As Row 1
Row 6: As Row 2
Row 7: Purl
Row 8: Knit

### Next row: decrease
k1, ssk, k1, k2 tog, yo, * k1, yo, ssk, k1, k2 tog, ssk, k1, k2 tog, yo; rep from * to the last 7 sts; k1, yo, ssk, k1, k2 tog, k1. 65/65/74 sts.
Work rows 2 to 6 of patt as before, but having 1 st less at each side of chevrons.
Change to 3¼mm needles and k1, p1 rib for 2 rows (1st and 2nd sizes having a k st at each end of right side rows).

### Next row: make eyelets
* k1, p1, yo, k2 tog; rep from * to the last 1/1/2 sts; rib 1/1/2.
Rib for a further 4 rows.
Cast off all sts loosely and evenly.

## FINISHING
To block and press see Guide to Techniques.
Join back and front at shoulder seams.
Pin collar evenly around neck, and stitch fairly loosely on the inside.
Sew up side and sleeve seam.
Insert sleeves, easing in evenly around armhole.
With 3.50mm crochet hook and MS, work 2 rows of DC around neck opening including collar ends.
Using 2 strands of MS, make a cord and thread through eyelets (to make cords see Guide to Techniques.)
Using 3 strands of contrast colours make a cord and thread through waist eyelets.
Using 2 strands of contrast colours make 2 cords and thread through wrist eyelets.
With MS make 2 pom-poms (diameter of card 2cm [¾in]) and attach to each end of neck tie (to make pom-poms see Guide to Techniques.)
With MS and all contrasts make 2 pom-poms (diameter of card 2½cm [1in]) and attach to each end of waist cord.
With MS and all contrasts make 4 pom-poms (diameter of card 1.5cm [½in]) and attach to each end of wrist cords.

# 5

# WARMER SEAS
# The Mediterranean

◇

# France

Girl's camisole (ages 2–13)

> *I should like to rise and go*
> *Where the golden apples grow –*
> *Where below another sky*
> *Parrot islands anchored lie.*

A cotton camisole for hot summer days, featuring a travelling vine pattern.

**SIZES**
Approx age: 2–3/4–5/6–7/8–9/10–11/12–13 years
To fit chest: 56/61/66/71/76/80cm (22/24/26/28/30/31½in)
Length (top of bodice to hem): 24/27/30/33/36/38cm (9½/10½/11¾/13/14¼/15in)

**YARN**
2/3/3/3/4/4 50g balls of fine cotton yarn
The yarn used in this garment is Pingouin Fil d'Ecosse no.5 in Ecru

**NEEDLES**
1 pair each 2¼mm and 2¾mm needles
2.50mm crochet hook

**NOTIONS**
6/6/7/8/9/10 Buttons

**TENSION**
34 sts and 44 rows to 10cm (4in) measured over st.st. using 2¾mm needles.

**CAMISOLE**
With 2¾mm needles, cast on 188/204/220/236/252/268 sts.
Patt as follows:
Row 1: (right side) k2, * yo, k1–b, yo, ssk, k5; rep from *, end k2
Row 2: p6, * p2 tog–b, p7; rep from *, end last rep with p5

Row 3: k2, * yo, k1–b, yo, k2, ssk, k3; rep
from *, end k2
Row 4: p4, * p2 tog–b, p7; rep from *
Row 5: k2, * k1–b, yo, k4, ssk, k1, yo; rep
from *, end k2
Row 6: p3, * p2 tog–b, p7; rep from *, end p1
Row 7: k2, * k5, k2 tog, yo, k1–b, yo; rep
from *, end k2
Row 8: p5, * p2 tog, p7; rep from *, end last
rep with p6
Row 9: k2, * k3, k2 tog, k2, yo, k1–b, yo; rep
from *, end k2
Row 10: * p7, p2 tog; rep from *, end p4
Row 11: k2, * yo, k1, k2 tog, k4, yo, k1–b;
rep from *, end k2
Row 12: p1, * p7, p2 tog; rep from *, end p3.
Repeat rows 1 to 12.
Continue in patt until piece measures 6/7/8/9/
10/10cm (2½/2¾/3/3½/4/4in) from beg, with right
side facing for next row.
Change to 2¼mm needles and work in k1, p1
rib for 4/4/6/6/6/6 rows.

### Next row: make eyelets
K1, * k2, yo, k2 tog; rep from *, end k3.
Rib for a further 5/5/7/7/7/7 rows.
Change to 2¾mm needles and work in patt as
before until piece measures 24/27/30/33/36/
38cm (9½/10½/11¾/13/14¼/15in) from beg, with
right side facing for next row.
Cast off evenly.


### FINISHING
To block and press see Guide to Techniques.

### Edging
With right side facing, 2.50mm crochet hook,
and beginning at bottom right front, work 1
row DC up right front, along top and down
left front.

### Next row: make eyelets and buttonholes
DC up left front, * 1 DC in each of next 2
DC, 2ch, miss 1 DC; rep from * along top, for
eyelets. Make buttonholes down right front: 2
DC, * 3 ch, miss 1 DC, DC into each of next 5
DC; rep from * to top of rib, DC to hem.

### Next row: picot edging
* 1 DC in each of next 3 DC, 3 ch, ss in first
ch; rep from * up right front (working DCs
into buttonhole ch), along top and down left
front.
Fasten off.

### Straps
With 2.50mm crochet hook, make a chain
24/27/29/32/34/37cm (9½/10½/11½/12½/13½/14½in)
long.
Work 2 rows DC into chain, then work 1 row
picot edging as body.
Attach straps with picot edgings facing
outwards.
Sew on buttons to correspond with
buttonholes.
Using 2 strands of yarn make a cord and
thread through waist eyelets. Make another
cord and thread through top eyelets. To make
cords, see Guide to Techniques.

# Spain

### Girl's blouse (ages 2–13)

A flamenco style blouse in Spanish lace. The diagonal Madeira stitch lends itself
well to knitting in the round.

## SIZES
Approx age: 2–3/4–5/6–7/8–9/10–11/12–13
years
To fit chest: 56/61/66/71/76/80cm (22/24/26/28/
30/31½in)
Length: 31/34/38/40/44/46cm (12/13½/15/16/
17½/18in)

## YARN
4/5/5/6/6/7 50g balls of fine cotton yarn
The yarn used in this garment is Pingouin Fil
d'Ecosse no.5 in Rose

## NEEDLES
1 set of 4 or circular 3mm, 2¾mm and 2¼mm
needles
NB If using circular needles then 1 pair of
2¾mm needles will also be required to work
back and front from armholes
2.50mm crochet hook

## NOTIONS
Shirring elastic.

## TENSION
16 sts and 22 rows to 5cm (2in) measured over
st.st. using 2¾mm needles.

## BODY
With 3mm needles cast on 228/244/260/272/
288/304 sts in the round.
NB Mark the first st with a contrast yarn, and
continue to mark this st every few rows.
Purl 1 round.
Change to 2¾mm needles and patt as follows:
Round 1: Knit
Round 2: * yo, sl1 – k2 tog – psso, yo, k1; rep
from * to end of round
Round 3: Knit
Round 4: * k1, yo, sl1 – k2 tog – psso, yo; rep
from * to end of round
Round 5: Knit
Round 6: Sl the first st back on to right hand
needle next to last st; * yo, k1, yo, sl1 – k2
tog – psso; rep from * to end of round
Round 7: Knit
Round 8: Sl the last st onto left hand needle;
* sl1 – k2 tog – psso, yo, k1, yo; rep from *
to end of round.
Repeat rounds 1 to 8 until piece measures
6/7/8/9/10/10cm (2½/2¾/3/3½/4/4in) from beg,
ending with a knit round for next round.

**Decrease for waist: 1st, 2nd and 3rd sizes only**
(k2 tog, k2) to the last 4 sts; k4. 172/184/196 sts.

**Decrease for waist: 4th, 5th, and 6th sizes only**
(k2 tog, k2) to end of round. 204/216/228 sts.

**All sizes**
Change to 2¼mm needles and k1, p1 rib for
2/2/3/3/3/3cm (¾/¾/1¼/1¼/1¼/1¼in).

**Increase: 1st, 2nd and 3rd sizes only**
(rib 3, m1) to the last 4 sts; rib 4. 228/244/260 sts.

**Increase: 4th, 5th, and 6th sizes only**
(rib 3, m1) to end of round. 272/288/304 sts.

**All sizes**
Change to 2¾mm needles and continue in patt as before until body measures 22/24/27/29/32/33cm (8¾/9½/10½/11½/12½/13in) from beg, ending after a knit round.

**Divide for armholes**
Cast off the first 6/7/7/7/8/8 sts, patt the next 108/115/123/129/136/144 sts and place on a spare needle, cast off the next 6/7/7/7/8/8 sts, and patt the rem 108/115/123/129/136/144 sts. Turn, and working on 2 needles, p2 tog, p 104/111/119/125/132/140, p2 tog.
Continue in patt, working rows 1, 3, 5 and 7 in purl on the wrong side, and decreasing 1 st at each end of wrong side rows until 94/99/105/109/114/120 sts remain.
Continue straight in patt until armhole measures 6/7/7.5/8/9/9.5cm (2½/2¾/3/3¼/3½/3¾in), with wrong side facing for next row.
Decrease as follows:
p 1/0/0/1/0/0, (p2 tog, p1) to end of row. 64/66/70/74/76/80 sts.
Place these sts on a spare needle.
With wrong side facing, purl the sts on the rem spare needle, decreasing 1 st at each end row.

Turn and patt as previous side, and work the final decrease row as previous side.
Place the sts on a spare needle.

**COLLAR**
With 3mm needles cast on 296/230/344/368/392/416 sts.
Purl 1 round.
Change to 2¾mm needles and patt as body until collar measures 8/8/9/10/11.5/12cm (3/3/3½/4/4½/4¾in), with a knit round for next round.
Decrease as follows:
(k2 tog, k1) to the last 2 sts; k2. 200/216/232/248/264/280 sts.

**Next round: join collar to body**
K the first 36/42/46/50/56/60 sts of collar, then with right side of body facing, place the sts from one spare needle behind the collar sts and knit together the next 64/66/70/74/76/80 sts of collar and the sts from spare needle, k the next 36/42/46/50/56/60 sts of collar, then placing the sts from rem spare needle behind the rem sts of collar, knit these sts together as previous side.
Change to 2¼mm needles and k1, p1 rib for 3cm (1¼in).
Cast off evenly in rib.

**FINISHING**
To block and press see Guide to Techniques. Thread several rounds of shirring elastic round the inside of collar rib.

# Italy

## Girl's party dress (ages 4–9)

Mediterranean chic in cool summer colours. A party dress featuring several famous Italian lace patterns, including a triple chevron border and lace medallions.

**SIZES**
Approx age: 4–5/6–7/8–9 years
To fit chest: 61/66/71cm (24/26/28in)
Length from top of shoulder: 53/57/64cm (21/22½/25¼in)
Sleeve seam: 10/11.5/13cm (4/4½/5in)

**YARN**
6/7/8 50g balls of fine cotton yarn
The yarn used in this garment is Pingouin Fil d'Ecosse no.5 in Ondine

**NEEDLES**
1 pair each 2¼mm and 2¾mm needles
2.50mm crochet hook

**NOTIONS**
3 metres of 0.5cm width ribbon
3 buttons

**TENSION**
16 sts and 22 rows to 5cm (2in) measured over st.st using 2¾mm needles.

**BACK**
** With 2¾mm needles cast on 205/217/229 sts.
Knit 4 rows.
Next row: (right side) * k2 tog, yo; rep from *

to the last st; k1.
Knit 3 rows, then work 4 rows in st.st
Now patt as follows:
Row 1: (right side) * k1, yo, ssk, k7, k2 tog, yo; rep from * to the last st; k1
Row 2 and all wrong side rows: Purl
Row 3: * k2, yo, ssk, k5, k2 tog, yo, k1; rep from * to the last st; k1
Row 5: * k1, (yo, ssk) twice, k3, (k2 tog, yo) twice; rep from * to the last st; k1
Row 7: * k2, (yo, ssk) twice, k1, (k2 tog, yo) twice, k1; rep from * to the last st; k1
Row 9: * k1, (yo, ssk) twice, yo, sl2 knitwise – k1 – p2sso, yo, (k2 tog, yo) twice; rep from * to the last st; k1
Row 11: As row 7
Row 13: * k3, yo, ssk, yo, sl2 knitwise – k1 – p2sso, yo, k2 tog, yo, k2; rep from * to the last st; k1
Row 15: * k4, yo, ssk, k1, k2 tog, yo, k3; rep from * to the last st; k1
Row 17: * k5, yo, sl2 knitwise – k1 – p2sso, yo, k4; rep from * to the last st; k1
Row 19: As row 2.
Work 12/14/16 rows in st.st.
Work the 18 patt rows again, then work 12/14/16 rows in st.st.
Work the 18 patt rows once more, then continue straight in st.st. until skirt measures 19/20/23cm (7½/8/9in), with right side facing for next row.
Decrease skirt as follows:
K 1/3/5, * k2 tog; rep from * to the last 0/2/4

sts; k 0/2/4. 103/111/119 sts.
Knit 3 rows.

**Next row: make eyelets**
* k2 tog, yo; rep from * to the last st; k1.
Knit 3 rows.
Now patt as follows:
Row 1: (right side) k 35/39/43, * k3, k2 tog,
  yo, k1, yo, ssk, k3; rep from * 2 more
  times; k 35/39/43
Row 2: p 35/39/43, * p2, p2 tog–b, yo, p3, yo,
  p2 tog, p2; rep from * 2 more times; p
  35/39/43
Row 3: k 35/39/43, * k1, (k2 tog, yo) twice,
  k1, (yo, ssk) twice, k1; rep from * 2 more
  times; k 35/39/43
Row 4: p 35/39/43, * (p2 tog–b, yo) twice, p3,
  (yo, p2 tog) twice; rep from * 2 more times;
  p 35/39/43
Row 5: k 35/39/43, * k1, (yo, ssk) twice, k1,
  (k2 tog, yo) twice, k1; rep from * 2 more
  times; k 35/39/43
Row 6: p 35/39/43, * p2, yo, p2 tog, yo, p3
  tog, yo, p2 tog–b, yo, p2; rep from * 2 more
  times; p 35/39/43
Row 7: k 35/39/43, * k3, yo, ssk, k1, k2 tog,
  yo, k3; rep from * 2 more times; k 35/39/43
Row 8: p 35/39/43, * p4, yo, p3 tog, yo, p4;
  rep from * 2 more times; p 35/39/43.
Continue in this manner, repeating rows 1 to
8 until back measures 21/23/26cm (8½/9/10¼in)
from skirt decrease row, with right side facing
for next row.

**Shape armholes**
Keeping continuity of patt, cast off 4/5/6 sts at
beg of next 2 rows.
Decrease 1 st at each end of the next 4 rows.
Patt 1 row straight then decrease 1 st at each
end of next and every foll alt row until 75/79/
83 sts remain. **
Continue straight in patt until armhole
measures 10.5/11.5/12.5cm (4/4½/5in) from
cast off, with right side facing for next row.

**Shape neck/right shoulder**
Knit 23/24/25 sts. Place the rem sts on a spare
needle.

Turn, p2 tog, p to end of row.
Continue in st.st, decreasing 1 st at neck edge
of wrong side rows until 18/19/20 sts remain.

**Next row: shape shoulder**
With right side facing, cast off 6 sts, k to end
of row.
Purl 1 row.
Repeat the last 2 rows once more.
Cast off the rem 6/7/8 sts.

**Shape neck/left shoulder**
With right side facing, place the next (centre)
29/31/33 sts on a length of yarn for back neck.
Rejoin yarn to the rem 23/24/25 sts and k to
end of row. Then work as right neck/
shoulder, reversing all shapings.

**FRONT**
As back from ** to **.
Continue straight in patt until armhole
measures 9/10/11cm (3½/4/4½in) from cast off,
with right side facing for next row.

**Shape neck/left shoulder**
Patt 25/26/27 sts. Place the rem sts on a spare
needle.
Turn, p2 tog, p to end of row.
Continue in patt decreasing 1 st at neck edge
of wrong side rows until 18/19/20 sts remain.
Continue straight until armhold corresponds
in length with back armhole at shoulder, with
right side facing for next row.
Shape shoulder as back.

**Shape neck/right shoulder**
With right side facing, place the next 25/27/29
sts on a length of yarn for front neck.
Rejoin yarn to the rem 25/26/27 sts, patt to
end of row. Then work as left neck/shoulder,
reversing all shapings.

**SLEEVES**
With 2¾mm needles cast on 71/75/79 sts.
Knit 4 rows.

**Next row: make eyelets**
* k2 tog, yo; rep from * to the last st; k1.

Knit 3 rows.
Continue in st.st. for 11 rows, ending with wrong side facing for next row.
Knit 3 rows.

### Next row: make eyelets
* k2 tog, yo; rep from * to the last st; k1.
Knit 3 rows.
Continue in st.st. until sleeve measures 10/11.5/13cm (4/4½/5in) from beg, with right side facing for next row.

### Shape top
Cast off 4/5/6 sts at beg of next 2 rows.
Work 2/4/6 rows straight, then decrease 1 st at each end of next and every foll alt row until 25 sts remain.
Decrease 1 st at each end of next and every foll row until 11 sts remain.
Cast off 3 sts at beg of next rows.
Cast off the rem 5 sts.

### FINISHING
To block and press see Guide to Techniques.
Join back and front at left shoulder seam.

### Neck
With 2¼mm needles, right side facing, and beginning at right back neck, knit up 9 sts down right back neck, pick up and knit the 29/31/33 sts of back neck, knit up 9 sts up left back neck, knit up 12 sts down left front neck, pick up and knit the 25/27/29 sts of front neck, knit up 12 sts up right front neck. 96/100/104 sts.
Knit 3 rows.

### Next row: make eyelets
* k2 tog, yo; rep from * to the last 2 sts; k2 tog.
Knit 4 rows.
Cast off evenly.
Sew up side and sleeve seams.
Insert sleeves, easing in any fullness around top.
Thread ribbon through eyelets above skirt, around neck, and sleeves.
With 2.50mm crochet hook, work 2 rows of DC along right shoulder opening, making 3 buttonholes at front of opening, on the last round. Sew on buttons to correspond with buttonholes.

# 6
## LOOKING EASTWARDS
## Eastern Europe

◇

# Bulgaria

Girl's sweater (ages 8–13)

> *On we rode, the others and I,*
> *Over the mountains blue, and by*
> *The Silver River, the sounding sea,*
> *And the robber woods of Tartary.*

For the competent knitter, a highly unusual, asymmetric pattern that is easier to work than it looks. The yoke on back and front is more complex and uses the Jacquard method. Inspiration courtesy of child's sock from Bulgaria.

**SIZES**
Approx age: 8–9/10–11/12–13 years
To fit chest: 71/76/80cm (28/30/31½in)
Length from top of shoulder: 46/49/52cm (18¼/19¼/20½in)
Sleeve seam: 32.5/34/35.5cm (12¾/13½/14in)

**YARN**
4/5/5 50g balls of DK yarn in MS
3/3/4 50g balls of same in 1st C
2 50g balls of same in 2nd C
1 50g ball of same in 3rd C
The yarn used in this garment is Emu Superwash DK in the following shades:
MS – Black; 1st C – Mulberry; 2nd C – Muscatel; 3rd C – Aran White

**NEEDLES**
1 pair each 3¼mm and 4mm needles

**TENSION**
25 sts and 25 rows to 10cm (4in) measured over chart A patt, using 4mm needles.

**BACK**
** With 3¼mm needles and MS, cast on 84/88/92 sts.
K1, p1 rib for 5/6/6cm (2/2½/2½in).

**Next row: increase**
Rib 6/2/4, (m1, rib 6) 12/14/14 times, m1, rib 6/2/4. (97/103/107 sts).
Change to 4mm needles and joining in 1st C,

**Chart A**

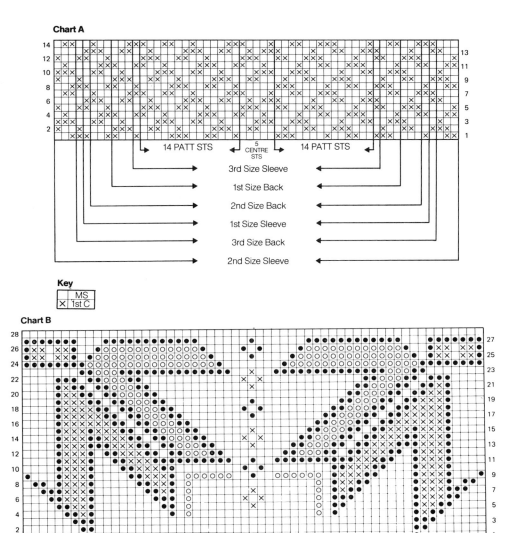

14 PATT STS ← 5 CENTRE STS → 14 PATT STS

3rd Size Sleeve

1st Size Back

2nd Size Back

1st Size Sleeve

3rd Size Back

2nd Size Sleeve

**Key**

| | MS |
|---|---|
| X | 1st C |

**Chart B**

57 PATT STS

**Key**

| | 2nd C |
|---|---|
| ● | MS |
| O | 3rd C |
| X | 1st C |

work the patt from chart A as follows:
Work the 4/7/9 edge sts, repeat the next 14
patt sts 3 times, work the centre 5 sts, repeat
the next 14 patt sts 3 times, work the 4/7/9
edge sts, as indicated.
Continue in this manner, repeating the 14
patt rows until back measures 31/32.5/34cm
(12¼/12¾/13½in) from beg, with right side
facing for next row.

**Shape armholes**
Break off MS and 1st C
With 2nd C, cast off the first 4/5/6 sts, k to
end of row.
Next row: cast off the first 4/5/6 sts, p to end
of row.

**Work yoke**
Wind off several lengths of each colour onto

97

bobbins (see Guide to Techniques for bobbins and Jacquard knitting).

Work the patt from chart B, placing the 57 patt sts in the centre of garment i.e. working 16/18/19 sts in st.st. at each side.

Continue in this manner, working all 28 rows of patt.

Break off MS, 1st C, and 3rd C yarns. **

With 2nd C, continue straight in st.st. until armhole measures 15/16.5/18cm (6/6½/7in), with right side facing for next row.

### Shape shoulder/neck

Cast off 8 sts, knit 16/17/17. Place the rem sts on a spare needle.

Turn and purl to end of row.

Next row: cast off 8 sts, k to end of row.

Purl 1 row, then cast off the rem 8/9/9 sts.

Place the next (centre) 41/43/45 sts on a length of yarn for back neck.

With right side facing, rejoin 2nd C and k the rem 24/25/25 sts.

Turn, and shape shoulder as previous, reversing shaping.

### FRONT

As back from ** to **.

With 2nd C, work 2/4/6 rows in st.st.

### Shape shoulder/neck

With right side facing, k 24/25/25 sts. Place the rem sts on a spare needle.

Turn, and work these 24/25/25 sts until armhole corresponds in length with back at shoulder, with right side facing for next row.

Cast off shoulder as back.

Place the next (centre) 41/43/45 sts on a length of yarn for front neck.

With right side facing, rejoin 2nd C and k the rem 24/25/25 sts.

Turn and work as previous, reversing shoulder shaping.

### SLEEVES

With 3¼mm needles and MS, cast on 40/44/46 sts. K1, p1 rib for 5/6/6cm (2/2½/2½in).

**Next row: increase**

### 1st and 2nd sizes

Rib 2, k twice into every st, to the last st, rib 1. 77/85 sts.

### 3rd size

Rib 1, k twice into every st to end of row. 91 sts.

### All sizes

Change to 4mm needles and joining in 1st C, work the patt from chart A as follows:

Work the 8/12/1 edge sts, repeat the next 14 patt sts 2/2/3 times, work the 5 centre sts, repeat the next 14 patt sts 2/2/3 times, work the 8/12/1 edge sts, as indicated.

Continue in this manner, repeating the 14 patt rows until sleeve measures 34/36/38cm (13½/14¼/15in) from beg, with right side facing for next row.

Cast off all sts.

### FINISHING

To block and press see Guide to Techniques.

Join back and front at shoulder seams.

### Neck

With 3¼mm needles and MS, pick up and k1, p1 rib the 41/43/45 sts of back neck.

Next row: k1, p2 tog, rib to the last 3 sts, p2 tog, k1

Next row: k1, rib to the last st, k1

Next row: k1, k2 tog, rib to the last 3 sts, k2 tog, k1

Next row: k1, rib to the last st, k1

Repeat these 4 rows, working 8/8/10 rows altogether.

Cast off evenly in rib.

Pick up the sts of front neck and work as back neck.

With 3¼mm needles, MS, and right side facing, knit up 19/21/23 sts along right side of neck. Work as back and front, and cast off evenly in rib.

Work the left side of neck in the same manner.

Stitch each corner seam of neck.

Insert sleeves, placing centre of sleeve at shoulder seam.

Sew up side and sleeve seams.

# Yugoslavia

## Boy's or girl's sweater (ages 6–11)

> *Whenever the moon and stars are set,*
> *Whenever the wind is high,*
> *All night long in the dark and wet,*
> *A man goes riding by.*

A sweater for when the wind is high, for both boys and girls. The original patterns and colours of a Yugoslavian sock have been translated into this warm sweater. The cream colour is embroidered on using the Swiss darning method. Another interesting design for the competent knitter.

### SIZES
Approx age: 6–7/8–9/10–11 years
To fit chest: 66/71/76cm (26/28/30in)
Length from top of shoulder: 42/46/49cm (16½/18¼/19¼in)
Sleeve seam: 34/37/41cm (13¼/14½/16in)

### YARN
5/6/7 50g balls of DK yarn in MS
3/3/4 50g balls of DK yarn in 1st C
1 50g ball of DK yarn in 2nd C
The yarn used in this garment is Emu Superwash DK in the following shades:
MS – Chestnut; 1st C – Black; 2nd C – Aran White

### NEEDLES
1 pair each 3¼mm and 4mm needles

### TENSION
25 sts and 25 rows to 10cm (4in) measured over patt from chart C, using 4mm needles.

### BACK
** With 3¼mm needles and MS, cast on 80/84/88 sts.
K2, p2 rib for 5/6/6cm (2/2½/2½in).

**Next row: increase**
Rib 4/6/2, (m1, rib 9/6/6) 8/12/14 times, m1, rib 4/6/2. 89/97/103 sts.
Change to 4mm needles, and joining in 1st C, work the patt from chart A as follows:
Work the 1/5/8 edge sts, repeat the next 16 patt sts twice, work the 23 centre sts, repeat the next 16 patt sts twice, and work the 1/5/8 edge sts, as indicated.
Continue in this manner, repeating the 16 patt rows until back measures 27.5/31/32.5cm (10¾/12¼/12¾in) from beg, with right side facing for next row. **

### Shape armholes
Keeping continuity of patt, cast off 4 sts at beg of next 2 rows.
Work the patt from chart B as follows:
Work the 0/0/3 edge sts, repeat the next 4 patt sts 10/11/11 times, work the centre st, repeat

**Chart A**

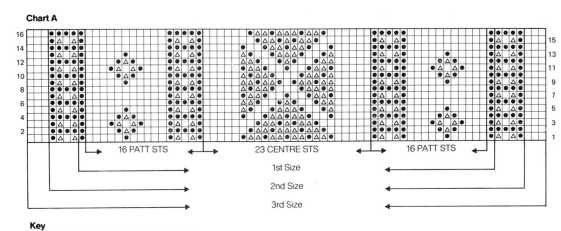

16 PATT STS | 23 CENTRE STS | 16 PATT STS

1st Size

2nd Size

3rd Size

**Key**

| | MS |
|---|---|
| △ | Work in MS: Swiss darn with 2nd C |
| ● | 1st C |

the next 4 patt sts 10/11/11 times, and work the 0/0/3 edge sts, as indicated.

Continue in this manner until armhole measures 14.5/15/16.5cm (5¾/6/6½in), with right side facing for next row.

## Shape shoulders

Keeping continuity of patt, cast off 8/9/10 sts at beg of next 2 rows.

Cast off 9/9/10 sts at beg of next 2 rows.

Cast off 9/10/10 sts at beg of next 2 rows.

Place the rem 29/33/35 sts on a length of yarn for back neck.

**Key**

| | MS |
|---|---|
| ● | 1st C |

**Chart B**

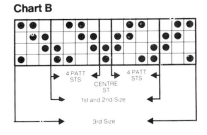

4 PATT STS | CENTRE ST | 4 PATT STS

1st and 2nd Size

3rd Size

## FRONT

As back from ** to **.

## Shape left armhole/side

Keeping continuity of patt, cast off the first 4 sts, patt 26/28/30 sts.

Place the rem sts on a spare needle.

Turn, and patt 1 row straight.

Now patt left side as follows:

Row 1: k 2/0/2 – MS, * k2 – 1st C, k2 – MS; rep from * to end

Row 2: p1 – 1st C, p2 – MS, p1 – 1st C; rep to the last 2/0/2 sts; p1 – 1st C, p 1/0/1 – MS

Row 3: k 2/0/2 – 1st C, * k2 – MS, k2 – 1st C; rep from * to end

Row 4: p1 – MS, p2 – 1st C, p1 – MS; rep to the last 2/0/2 sts; p 1/0/1 – MS, p 1/0/1 – 1st C.

Repeat these 4 rows until armhole measures 14.5/15/16.5cm (5¾/6/6½in), with right side facing for next row.

## Shape shoulder

Keeping continuity of patt, cast off 8/9/10 sts, patt to end.

Patt 1 row straight.

Cast off 9/9/10 sts, patt to end.

Patt 1 row straight, then cast off the rem 9/10/10 sts.

## Neck opening/right side

With right side facing and MS, cast off the next (centre) 29/33/35 sts.

Join in 1st C, and keeping continuity of chart A patt, work to end of row.

## Shape armhole

Cast off 4 sts, patt to end.

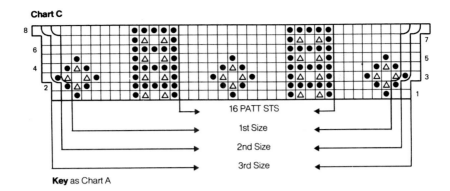

**Chart C**

16 PATT STS

1st Size

2nd Size

3rd Size

**Key** as Chart A

Now patt right side as follows:

Row 1: k2 – MS, k2 – 1st C; rep to the last
2/0/2 sts; k 2/0/2 – MS

Row 2: p 1/0/1 – MS, p 1/0/1 – 1st C, * p1 – 1st
C, p2 – MS, p1 – 1st C; rep from * to end

Row 3:* k2 – 1st C, k2 – MS; rep to the last
2/0/2 sts; k 2/0/2 – 1st C

Row 4: p 1/0/1 – 1st C, p 1/0/1 – MS,* p1 –
MS, p2 – 1st C, p1 – MS; rep from * to end.

Repeat these 4 rows until armhole measures
14.5/15/16.5cm (5¾/6/6½in), with wrong side
facing for next row.

Shape shoulder as left side.

## SLEEVES

With 3¼mm needles cast on 40/42/44 sts.
K2, p2 rib (2nd size having a k2 at each end of
right side rows) for 5/6/6cm (2/2½/2½in).

**Next row: increase**

Rib 4/1/2, (m1, rib 4/5/5) 8 times, m1, rib
4/1/2. 49/51/53 sts.

Change to 4mm needles, and joining in 1st C,
work the patt from chart C, repeating the 16
patt sts twice, and working the first 6/7/8 sts
and the last 11/12/13 sts on k rows, and the
first 11/12/13 sts and the last 6/7/8 sts on p
rows, as indicated.

Continue in this manner, repeating the 8 patt
rows and increasing 1 st at each end of 3rd
and every foll 6th row (working increased sts
into patt) until there are 73/77/83 sts.

Continue straight in patt until sleeve
measures 35.5/38.5/42.5cm (14/15¼/16¾in)
from beg, with right side facing for next row.
With MS cast off all sts.

## FINISHING

To block and press see Guide to Techniques.
With 2nd C, and working the patt sections
from the top downwards, Swiss darn the sts
indicated on charts A and C (see Guide to
Techniques for Swiss darning).
Join back and front at shoulder seams.

**Collar**

With right side facing, 3¼mm needles, and
MS, and beginning at centre back neck, pick
up and knit 15/17/18 sts towards left shoulder,
knit up 39/41/44 sts down left front opening.
Work in k2, p2 rib until collar fits across front
neck opening.
Cast off evenly in rib.
With right side facing, 3¼mm needles, and
MS, knit up 40/42/45 sts up right front neck,
pick up and knit the rem 14/16/17 sts of back
neck.
Work as left collar.
Sew up centre back collar seam.
Stitch collar across front opening, crossing
right over left.
Place centre of sleeve at shoulder seam and
sew in sleeve.
Sew up side and sleeve seams.

# 7

## FARTHER AND FARTHER

◇

# Arabia

Boy's or girl's sweater (ages 2–13)

> *Where in sunshine reaching out,*
> *Eastern cities, miles about,*
> *Are with mosque and minaret*
> *Among sandy gardens set.*
> *And the rich goods from near and far*
> *Hang for sale in the bazaar.*

The home of the oldest known knitted samples. The ancient twisted technique is put to effect in this casual raglan sweater, in a desert shade of cotton.

### SIZES
Approx age: 2–3/4–5/6–7/8–9/10–11/12–13 years
To fit chest: 56/61/66/71/76/80cm (22/24/26/28/30/31½)
Length from back neck: 34/38/42/46/49/52.5cm (13½/15/16½/18/19¼/20¾in)
Sleeve seam: 23/27/31/34/38/41cm (9/10½/12¼/13½/15/16in)

### YARN
6/6/7/8/9/10 50g balls of DK cotton yarn
The yarn used in this garment is Pingouin Coton Naturel 8 Fils in Ecru.

### NEEDLES
1 pair each 3¼mm and 4mm needles

### TENSION
23 sts and 28 rows to 10cm (4in) measured in twisted st.st. using 4mm needles
Work twisted st.st. thus: Right side rows: sl1; k–b to end of row.
Wrong side rows: purl.

### BACK
** With 3¼mm needles cast on 62/67/72/77/82/87 sts.
K1, p1 rib for 5/5.5/6/6/7/7cm (2/2¼/2½/2½/2¾/2¾in), (2nd, 4th, and 6th sizes having a k st at each end of right side rows).

**Next row: increase**
Rib 4/3/3/2/2/1, (m1, rib 6) 9/10/11/12/13/14 times, m1, rib 4/4/3/3/2/2. 72/78/84/90/96/102 sts.

Change to 4mm needles and work Twisted Pennant patt as follows:

Row 1: (right side) sl1, p5, * k1–b, p5; rep from * to end of row

Row 2: * k4, p2–b; rep from * to the last 6 sts; k4, p1–b, k1

Row 3: sl1, k2–b, p3, * k3–b, p3; rep from * to end of row

Row 4: * k2, p4–b; rep from * to the last 6 sts; k2, p3–b, k1

Row 5: sl1, k4–b, p1, * k5–b, p1; rep from * to end of row

Row 6: As row 4

Row 7: As row 3

Row 8: As row 2.

Repeat these 8 rows until back measures 20/23/25.5/28/30.5/33cm (8/9/10/11/12/13in) from beg, with right side facing for next row.

### Shape armholes

Cast off the first 2/2/3/3/4/4 sts; k–b to end of row.

Next row: Cast off the first 2/2/3/3/4/4 sts; p to end of row.

### Shape raglan

Row 1: (right side) sl1; k–b to end of row

Row 2: sl1 purlwise, p2 tog; p to the last 3 sts; p2 tog–b, p1. **

Repeat these 2 rows until 34/36/38/40/42/44 sts remain, with right side facing for next row.

### Shape neck

sl1, k6–b. Place the next 20/22/24/26/28/30 sts on a length of yarn for back neck. Place the rem sts on a spare needle.

Turn, and work the first 7 sts, decreasing 1 st at neck edge of first and every foll alt row, and at the same time continue to decrease at raglan edge as before. Continue in this manner until 3 sts remain.

Next row: sl1 – k2 tog – psso.

Break off yarn and thread through rem st to fasten off.

With right side facing, rejoin yarn to the rem 7 sts and k–b to end of row.

Turn and decrease at raglan as before, and at neck edge as previous side, until 3 sts remain.

Work final row and fasten off as previous side.

### FRONT

As back from ** to **.

Repeat these 2 rows until 42/44/48/50/52/54 sts remain, with right side facing for next row.

### Shape neck

sl1, k 14/14/16/16/16/16–b. Place the next 12/14/14/16/18/20 sts on a length of yarn for front neck. Place the rem sts on a spare needle.

Turn, and work the first 15/15/17/17/17/17 sts, decreasing 1 st at neck edge of first and foll alt rows, and at the same time continue to decrease at raglan edge as before. Continue in this manner until 3 sts remain.

Next row: sl1 – k2 tog – psso.

Break off yarn and thread through rem st to fasten off.

With right side facing, rejoin yarn to the rem 15/15/17/17/17/17 sts and k–b to end of row.

Turn, and decrease at raglan as before, and at neck edge as previous side, until 3 sts remain.

Work final row and fasten off as previous side.

### SLEEVES

With 3¼mm needles cast on 30/32/34/36/38/40 sts.

K1, p1 rib for 5/5.5/6/6/7/7cm (2/2¼/2½/2½/2¾/2¾in).

### Next row: increase

Rib 2/1/2/0/1/2, (m1, rib 5/6/6/7/7/7) 5 times, m1, rib 3/1/2/1/2/3. 36/38/40/42/44/46 sts.

Change to 4mm needles and work Twisted Pennant patt as follows:

**1st and 4th sizes** Work as back

**2nd and 5th sizes** Work as back, but omit the sl st on right side rows and work 1 extra st at each side into patt. (i.e. Row 1: p1, * k1–b, p5; rep from * to the last st; k1–b)

**3rd and 6th sizes** Work as back, but omit the sl st on right side rows and work 2 extra sts at each side into patt. (i.e. Row 1: p2, * k1–b, p5; rep from * to the last 2 sts; k1–b, p1).

**All sizes**

Continue in patt, increasing 1 st at each end of 3rd/5th/5th/4th/6th/6th row, and every foll 6th/6th/6th/7th/7th/7th row (working all increased sts into patt) until there are 50/54/58/62/66/70 sts.

Continue straight until sleeve measures 23/27/31/34/38/41cm (9/10½/12¼/13½/15/16in) from beg, with right side facing for next row.

**Shape armhole**

Cast off the first 2/2/3/3/4/4 sts; k–b to end of row.

Next row: Cast off the first 2/2/3/3/4/4 sts; p to end of row.

**Shape raglan**

Row 1: (right side) sl1; k–b to end of row

Row 2: sl1 purlwise, p2 tog; p to the last 3 sts; p2 tog–b, p1.

Repeat these 2 rows until 8 sts remain.

Place these sts on a length of yarn.

**FINISHING**

To block and press see Guide to Techniques.

Join back, front and sleeves at raglan seams, leaving back/left sleeve seam open.

**Neck**

With 3¼mm needles, pick up and knit the 8 sts of left sleeve, knit up 9/9/11/11/11/11 sts down left front neck, pick up and knit the 12/14/14/16/18/20 sts of front neck, knit up 9/9/11/11/11/11 sts up right front neck, pick up and knit the 8 sts of right sleeve, knit up 3 sts down right back neck, pick up and knit the 20/22/24/26/28/30 sts of back neck, knit up 3 sts up left back neck. 72/76/82/86/90/94 sts.

K1, p1 rib for 2/2/2.5/2.5/3/3cm (¾/¾/1/1/1¼/1¼in), with right side facing for next row.

Change to 4mm needles and work in st.st. for 3/3/4/4/5/5cm (1¼/1¼/1½/1½/2/2in) with right side facing for next row.

Cast off evenly.

Sew up remaining raglan seam and neck, stitching rib on the inside and st.st. on the k side.

Sew up side and sleeve seams.

# Inca Jacket

## Boy's or girl's jacket (ages 6–13)

> *While here at home, in shining day,*
> *We round the sunny garden play,*
> *Each little Indian sleepy-head*
> *Is being kissed and put to bed.*
>
> *And when at eve I rise from tea,*
> *Day dawns beyond the Atlantic Sea;*
> *And all the children in the west*
> *Are getting up and being dressed.*

The first of three designs inspired by Inca hats bought at the Indian market in La Paz, Bolivia. This mohair jacket features the Inca birds and geometric patterns.

## SIZES

Approx age: 6–7/8–9/10–11/12–13 years
To fit chest: 66/71/76/80cm (26/28/30/31½in)
Length from top of shoulder: 38/42/46/50cm (15/16½/18/19¾in)
Sleeve seam: 25/29/33/36cm (10/11½/13/14¼in)

## YARN

6/7/8/9 25g balls of mohair yarn in MS
1/2/2/2 25g balls of same in 1st C
1 25g ball of same in 2nd C
The yarn used in this garment is Emu Filigree in the following shades:
MS – Summer Navy; 1st C – Poppy; 2nd C – Electric blue

## NEEDLES

1 pair each 5mm and 5½mm needles

## NOTIONS

8/9/10/11 hooks and eyes

## TENSION

17 sts and 20 rows to 10cm (4in), measured over st.st. using 5½mm needles.

## BACK

With 5mm needles and 1st C, cast on 66/70/74/78 sts.
Work border as follows:
Row 1: * k2 – 1st C, k2 – 2nd C; rep from * to the last 2 sts; k2 – 1st C
Row 2: As row 1, but bringing the yarns to the front of work (wrong side)
Rows 3 and 4: With 1st C – knit.
Break off contrast yarns. Change to 5½mm needles and MS, and work straight in st.st.

**Chart A**

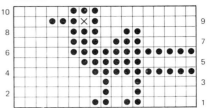

**Chart B**

**Key**

| | MS |
|---|---|
| × | 2nd C |
| ● | 1st C |

until back measures 22/25/28/31cm (8¾/9¾/ 11/12¼in) from beg, with right side facing for next row.

**Shape armholes**
Cast off 3/3/4/4 sts at beg of next 2 rows.
Continue straight until armhole measures 16/ 17/18/19cm (6¼/6¾/7/7½in), with right side facing for next row.
Place the first 19/20/20/21 sts on a holder (right shoulder), place the next 22/24/26/28 sts on a length of yarn (back neck), and place the rem 19/20/20/21 sts on a holder (left shoulder).

**RIGHT FRONT**
** With 5mm needles and 1st C, cast on 32/ 34/36/38 sts.
Work border as follows:
Row 1: * k2 – 1st C, k2 – 2nd C; rep from * to end of row
Row 2: * k2 – 2nd C yarn forward, k2 – 1st C yarn forward; rep from * to end of row
Rows 3 and 4: With 1st C – knit.
Break off contrast yarns. Change to 5½mm needles and MS and work in st.st. for 8/10/6/8 rows. **
With right side facing, and joining in colours as required, work the patt from chart A over the first 17 sts. Work all 10 rows of chart (carry the contrast yarn to st no.17 on rows 3 and 5, in order to position the yarn for working the birds tail).
Break off contrast yarns and with MS work

6/8/6/8 rows in st.st.
Repeat this sequence of 10 rows chart A, then 6/8/6/8 rows st.st., 2/2/3/3 more times (reverse the colours on each working of chart – see photograph). *At the same time*, when front corresponds with back at armhole, with wrong side facing for next row, shape armhole by casting off 3/3/4/4 sts at beg of row.
When 3/3/4/4 birds plus 6/8/6/8 rows of st.st. have been worked, then shape neck as follows:
With right side facing, k 5/6/7/8 sts and place on a safety pin (front neck), k to end of row. Continue in st.st. and decrease 1 st at neck edge of next 2 rows.
Work 1 row straight, then decrease 1 st at neck edge of next and every foll alt row until 19/20/20/21 sts remain.
Continue straight until armhole corresponds in length with back armhole, with right side facing for next row. Place the sts on a holder.

**LEFT FRONT**
As right front from ** to **.
With right side facing and joining in colours as required, work the patt from chart B over the last 17 sts. Work all 10 rows of chart, then break off contrast yarns and with MS, work in st.st. for 6/8/6/8 rows.
Repeat this sequence of 10 rows chart B, then 6/8/6/8 rows st.st. 2/2/3/3 more times, reversing the colours at each working of chart. Shape armhole and neck as right front, in reverse (shape neck after working the final

5/7/5/7 rows of st.st.). Place the shoulder sts on a holder.

## SLEEVES
With 5mm needles and 1st C, cast on 54/58/62/66 sts.
Work the 4 border rows as back.
Break off contrast yarns. Change to 5½mm needles and with MS, work straight in st.st. until sleeve measures 26.5/30.5/35/38cm (10½/11/13¾/15in).
Cast off evenly.

## FINISHING
With right sides of back and fronts together, knit together and cast off the sts of back and front shoulders, thus joining fronts to back. To block and press see Guide to Techniques.

### Armhole borders
With right side facing, 5mm needles and 1st C, knit up 50/54/58/62 sts.
Knit 1 row.
Work border as back from row 1 through 3.
With 1st C, cast off evenly.

### Neck border
With right side facing, 5mm needles, 1st C, and beg at right front, pick up and knit the 5/6/7/8 sts from safety pin, knit up 8 sts up right neck edge, pick up and knit the 22/24/26/28 sts of back neck, decreasing 1 st at each end, knit up 8 sts down left neck edge, and pick up and knit the 5/6/7/8 sts from safety pin. 46/50/54/58 sts.
Knit 1 row.
Work border as back from row 1 through 3.
With 1st C, cast off evenly.

### Front borders
With right side facing, 5mm needles, and 1st C, knit up 56/62/66/72 sts along each front edge.
Knit 1 row.

### 1st and 4th sizes only
Work border as right front from row 1 through 3.
Cast off evenly.

### 2nd and 3rd sizes only
Work border as back from row 1 through 3.
Cast off evenly.

Oversew cast off edge of sleeve to to wrong side of armhole, so that armhole border overlaps sleeve on the right side.
Sew each end of border and top of sleeve to armhole cast off.
Sew up side and sleeve seams.
Sew hooks and eyes to insides of front borders, spaced at even intervals from top to bottom.

# Bolivian Poncho

### Girl's poncho and hat (ages 2–7)

A childs' version of the famous garment from the Andes.

## SIZES
Approx age: 2–3/4–5/6–7 years
To fit chest: 56/61/66cm (22/24/26in)
Length from top of shoulder: 48/53/57cm (19/21/22½in)

## YARN
2/3/3 50g balls of Aran yarn in MS
2/3/4 50g balls of same in 1st C
2/3/4 50g balls of same in 2nd C
The yarn used in this garment is Emu Aran in the following shades:
MS – Natural; 1st C – Wine; 2nd C – Matelot

## NEEDLES
1 pair each 4½mm and 5mm needles

## TENSION
22 sts and 22 rows to 10cm (4in) measured over patt using 5mm needles.

## *PONCHO*

### BACK
With 4½mm needles and 1st C, cast on 98/106/114 sts.
Join in MS and patt border as follows:
Row 1: (right side) k2 – MS; k2 – 1st C; rep to the last 2 sts; k2 – MS
Row 2: As row 1 but bringing the yarns to the front of work (wrong side)
Rows 3 and 4: With MS, knit.

Break off 1st C, and with 2nd C increase as follows:
K 1/3/2, (m1, k 32/20/22) 3/5/5 times, m1, k 1/3/2. 102/112/120 sts.

### 3rd Size only
st.st. for 2 rows

### All sizes
Purl 1 row.
Change to 5mm needles, join in MS, and work the patt from chart A, repeating the 28 patt sts 3/4/4 times across, and working the first 18/0/8 sts on k rows, and the last 18/0/8 sts on p rows as indicated.
Change to 4½mm needles and with 2nd C, st.st. for 2/2/4 rows.
Then joining in and breaking off colours as required, work st.st. stripes as follows:
1 row in MS
2 rows in 1st C
1 row in MS
2 rows in 2nd C
1 row in MS
2/4/4 rows in 1st C.
Change to 5mm needles and with 1st C and MS, work the 11 rows of patt from chart B, repeating the 16 patt sts 6/7/7 times across, and working the first 6/0/8 sts on k rows, and the last 6/0/8 sts on p rows as indicated.
Change to 4½mm needles and with 1st C st.st. for 2/4/4 rows.
Then joining in and breaking off colours as required, work in st.st. stripes as follows:
1 row in MS
2 rows in 2nd C

**Chart A**

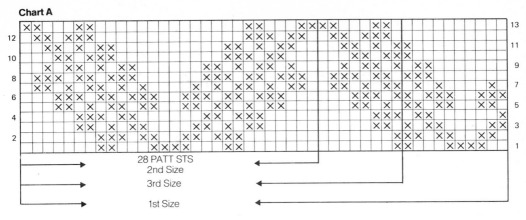

28 PATT STS
2nd Size

3rd Size

1st Size

**Key**

| ✕ | MS |
|---|----|
|   | 2nd C |

**Chart B**

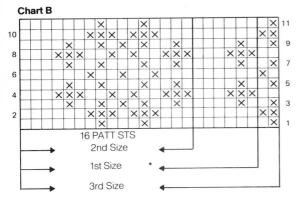

16 PATT STS
2nd Size

1st Size

3rd Size

**Key**

| ✕ | MS |
|---|----|
|   | 1st C |

**Chart C**

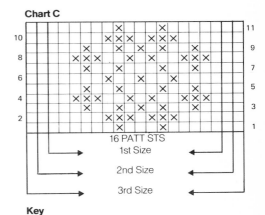

16 PATT STS
1st Size

2nd Size

3rd Size

**Key**

| ✕ | MS |
|---|----|
|   | 2nd C |

1 row in MS. **
3 rows in 1st C
1 row in MS
2 rows in 2nd C
1 row in MS
2/4/4 rows in 1st C.
Change to 5mm needles, and with 1st C and MS work the 11 rows of patt from chart B, as before.
Work 2/4/4 rows in 1st C.
Change to 4½mm needles and work in st.st. stripes as follows:
1 row in MS
2 rows in 2nd C
1 row in MS

2 rows in 1st C
1 row in MS
2/2/4 rows in 2nd C.
Change to 5mm needles and with 2nd C and MS, work the 13 rows of patt from chart A, as before.
Change to 4½mm needles and with 2nd C st.st. for 1/1/3 rows.

**Next row: decrease**
K 3/3/4, (k2 tog, k 30/19/20) 3/5/5 times, k2 tog, k 1/2/4. 98/106/114 sts.
Purl 1 row.
Work border as follows:
Rows 1 and 2: with MS – knit

113

Row 3: k2 – MS, k2 – 1st C; rep to the last 2 sts; k2 – MS

Row 4: As row 3 but bringing yarns to the front of work (wrong side)

Row 5: With 1st C – knit.

Cast off evenly in 1st C.

## FRONT

As back to end of row 4, chart B.

### Next row: shape left neck

With right side facing, cast off 2/3/3 sts at beg of next row, patt to end.

Keeping continuity of patt, decrease 1 st at end of next and same edge of every foll row, 4/5/6 times. 96/104/111 sts.

Continue working in stripes and changing needles as back, and work 1 row straight. Then decrease 1 st at neck edge of next and every foll alt row 3 times. 93/101/108 sts. Continue straight in stripes as back to **.

### Neck opening

With wrong side facing, and continuing in stripe sequence, work to the last 18/22/22 sts. Place these sts on a length of yarn.

Turn and work 1 row straight.

Work the next row, casting on 18/22/22 sts at neck edge.

### Shape right neck

Continue in patt and needle sequence as back, and shape neck as left neck in reverse i.e. increase and cast on at the appropriate patt row, ending neck shaping on row 7 of chart B. Continue in patt as back to end.

## FINISHING

Join back and front at shoulders, placing the incomplete chart patterns of back at shoulders.

### Neck

With 4½mm needles, MS, and beginning at right front neck, knit up 15/17/17 sts to shoulder seam, knit up 24/28/28 sts along back neck, knit up 15/17/17 sts down left front neck. 54/62/62 sts.

Knit 1 row.

Join in 2nd C and patt as follows:

Row 1: k2 – MS, k2 – 2nd C; rep to the last 2 sts; k2 – MS

Row 2: As row 1 but bringing the yarns to the front of work (wrong side)

Row 3: With 2nd C – knit.

Break off MS and with 2nd C cast off evenly.

### Right neck opening

With 4½mm needles and MS knit up 20/24/24 sts along right neck opening.

Knit 3 rows.

Cast off evenly.

### Left front opening

With 4½mm needles and MS, pick up and k the sts of left front opening as follows: k2 from neck border, pick up 18/22/22 sts from opening. 20/24/24 sts.

Knit 1 row.

Next row: k2 – MS, k2 – 2nd C; rep to end

Next row: k2 – 2nd C, k2 – MS; rep to end.

Break off MS and with 2nd C knit 1 row.

Cast off evenly in 2nd C.

### Hemline borders

With right side facing, 4½mm needles, and MS, knit up 98/106/110 sts.

Knit 1 row.

Next Row: k2 – MS, k2 – 1st C; rep to the last 2 sts; k2 – MS

Next Row: As previous row but bringing yarns to front of work (wrong side).

Break off MS and with 1st C knit 1 row.

Cast off evenly in 1st C.

## HAT

With 4½mm needles and 1st C, cast on 88/88/92 sts.

Next row: (right side) k2 – 1st C, k2 – MS; rep to end of row.

Next row: As previous row but bringing yarns to front of work (wrong side).

Break off 1st C, and with MS, k 2 rows.

Join in 2nd C and increase as follows:

K 2/3/0, (m1, k 12/9/13) 7/9/7 times, m1, k 2/4/1. 96/98/100 sts.

Purl 1 row.

**3rd size only**

st.st. for a further 2 rows

**All sizes**

Change to 5mm needles, and joining in MS, work the 11 rows of patt from chart C, repeating the 16 patt sts 6 times across, and working the first and last 0/1/2 sts on every row as indicated.

Change to 4½mm needles and with 2nd C, st.st. for 1/3/3 rows.

Continue in st.st. as follows:

1 row in MS
2 rows in 1st C
1 row in MS
1 row in 2nd C.

**Next row: decrease**

With 2nd C, p 3/4/0, (k2 tog, k8) to the last 3/4/0 sts; k 3/4/0. 87/89/90 sts.

Continue in stripe sequence as set, and work 4 rows.

**Next row: decrease**

k 3/4/0, (k2 tog, k7) to the last 3/4/0 sts; k 3/4/0. 78/80/80 sts. Work 3 rows.

**Next row: decrease**

k 3/0/0, (k2 tog, k6) to the last 3/0/0 sts; k 3/0/0. 69/70/70 sts.

Work 2 rows.

**Next row: decrease**

p 3/0/0. (p2 tog, p5) to the last 3/0/0 sts; p 3/0/0. 60 sts.

Break off MS and 1st C and continue with 2nd C and work 3 rows.

**Next row: decrease**

(p2 tog, p4) to end of row. 50 sts.
Work 1 row.

**Next row: decrease**

(p2 tog, p3) to end of row. 40 sts.
Work 1 row.

**Next row: decrease**

(p2 tog, p2) to end of row. 30 sts.
Work 1 row.

**Next row: decrease**

(p2 tog, p1) to end of row. 20 sts.
Next row: k2 tog to end of row. 10 sts.
Thread the yarn through the rem sts and fasten off.

**Earflaps (make 2)**

With 4½mm needles and 1st C, cast on 18 sts.
Patt as follows:

Row 1: k2 – 1st C, k2 – MS; rep to the last 2 sts; k2 – 1st C

Row 2: As row 1, but bringing the yarns to front of work (wrong side)

Row 3: With MS – k14, turn

Row 4: With MS – sl the first st, k to end of row

Row 5: With 2nd C – k12, turn

Row 6: With 2nd C – sl the first st, p to end of row

Row 7: With MS – k10, turn

Row 8: With MS – sl the first st, k to end of row

Row 9: With 1st C – k8, turn

Row 10: With 1st C – sl the first st, p to end of row

Rows 11 and 12: Rep rows 9 and 10

Row 13: With MS – k10, turn

Row 14: With MS – sl the first st, k to end of row

Row 15: With 2nd C – k12, turn

Row 16: With 2nd C – sl the first st, p to end of row

Row 17: With MS – k14, turn

Row 18: With MS – sl the first st, k to end of row

Row 19: As row 1

Row 20: As row 2.

Cast off evenly with 1st C.

**FINISHING**

Sew up centre back seam.

Using 1 strand of each colour plait 2 cords and attach to ends of earflaps.

Make another cord for top of hat, and 2 for neck opening.

Using MS, make 5 small tassels and attach to each cord.

Position the earflaps at each side of hat and sew on.

# Bolivian Catsuits

## Girl's all-in-one suits (ages 2–7)

*See photograph on front of jacket.*

What better than a catsuit to show off the Inca cat motifs found on another hat from the market in La Paz. Knitted in cotton with bright colours and geometric patterns.

## SIZES
Approx age: 2–3/4–5/6–7 years
To fit chest: 56/61/66cm (22/24/26in)
Back neck to crotch: 46/51/56cm (18/20/22in)
Inside leg (long): 35/42/48cm (13¾/16½/19in)
Inside leg (short): 11/13/15cm (4¼/5/6in)
Sleeve seam (long): 23/27/31cm (9/10½/12in)
Sleeve seam (short): 9.5/10/11cm (3¾/4/4¼in)

## YARN (Long Version)
6/7/7 50g balls of cotton DK yarn in MS
2/3/3 50g balls of same in 1st C
2 50g balls of same in 2nd C

## YARN (Short Version)
4/5/5 50g balls of cotton yarn in MS
1/2/3 50g balls of same in 1st C
1/2/2 50g balls of same in 2nd C
The yarn used here is Pingouin Coton Naturel
8 Fils, in Corrida, Floride, and Soliel

## NEEDLES
1 pair each 3¼mm and 4mm needles

## NOTIONS
30cm (12in) zip fastener; 12 beads

## TENSION
20 sts and 26 rows to 10cm (4in) measured over chart B, using 4mm needles.

## CATSUIT (Long Version)

### RIGHT LEG
With 3¼mm needles and MS, cast on 44/46/48 sts. K1, p1 rib for 5cm (2in).

**Next row: increase**
Rib 2/1/1, (m1, rib 2) 7/8/8 times, (m1, rib 1) 12/13/14 times, (m1, rib 2) 7/7/8 times, m1, rib 2/2/1. 71/75/79 sts.
Change to 4mm needles and work 2 rows st.st.
Work stripes as follows:
1 row 1st C/1 row 2nd C/2 rows MS.
Join in 1st C and work the patt from chart A, repeating the 16 patt sts 4 times across, and working the first 3/5/7 sts and the last 4/6/8 sts on k rows, and the first 4/6/8 sts and the last 3/5/7 sts on p rows as indicated.
Break off 1st C, and with MS st.st. for 2 rows.
Then joining in and breaking off colours as required, work the patt from chart B, repeating the 6 patt sts 11/12/13 times across, and working the first 2/1/0 sts and the last 3/2/1 sts on k rows, and the first 3/2/1 sts and the last 2/1/0 sts on p rows as indicated.
Continue in this manner until leg measures 24/28/34cm (9½/11/13½in) from beg, with right side facing for next row.

117

**Chart A**

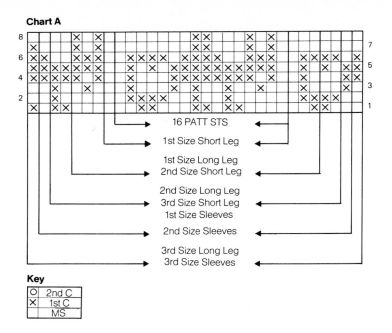

16 PATT STS

1st Size Short Leg

1st Size Long Leg
2nd Size Short Leg

2nd Size Long Leg
3rd Size Short Leg
1st Size Sleeves

2nd Size Sleeves

3rd Size Long Leg
3rd Size Sleeves

**Key**

| | |
|---|---|
| O | 2nd C |
| X | 1st C |
| | MS |

## Shape leg

Keeping continuity of patt, increase 1 st at end of next and foll 4th row.

Patt 3 rows straight, then increase 1 st at *each* end of next and every foll 4th row until there are 81/87/91 sts, working inc sts into patt. Continue straight in patt until leg measures 35/42/48cm (13¾/16½/19in) from beg, with right side facing for next row.

## ** Shape crotch

Keeping continuity of patt, cast off 2/3/3 sts, patt to end of row.

Next row: Cast off 3/3/4 sts, patt to end of row.

Decrease 1 st at each end of next 2 rows.

Next row: (right side facing) Patt to the last 2 sts, k2 tog.

Next row: p2 tog, patt to the last 2 sts, p2 tog.

Patt 1 row straight, then decrease 1 st at each end of the foll row. 67/72/75 sts.

Place the sts on a spare needle.

## LEFT LEG

As right leg, but reversing all shapings and ending on the same patt row.

## Join Legs

With right side facing, and keeping continuity of patt, work to the last st of right leg, then with right side of left leg facing, k together the last st of right leg and the first st of left

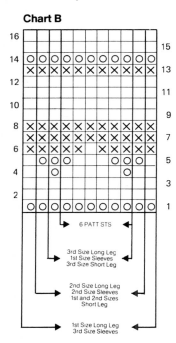

**Chart B**

6 PATT STS

3rd Size Long Leg
1st Size Sleeves
3rd Size Short Leg

2nd Size Long Leg
2nd Size Sleeves
1st and 2nd Sizes
Short Leg

1st Size Long Leg
3rd Size Sleeves

118

leg, patt to end of left leg. 133/143/149 sts.
Continue straight in patt until body measures
14/16/18cm (5½/6¼/7in) from *crotch cast off*,
with right side facing for next row.

### Decrease for waist
K 2/5/7, (k2 tog, k 5/4/4) to the last 5/6/10 sts;
k2 tog, k 3/4/8. 114/120/126 sts.
Change to 3¼mm needles and MS, and k1, p1
rib for 5 rows.

### Next row: make eyelets
Rib 2/1/2, (yo, k2 tog, rib 2) to the last 4/3/4
sts; yo, k2 tog, rib 2/1/2.
Rib for a further 4 rows.

### Next row: increase
Rib 3/5/8, (m1, rib 6/5/5) to the last 3/5/8 sts;
m1, rib 3/5/8. 133/143/149 sts.
Change to 4mm needles, and joining in and
breaking off colours as required, work the
patt from chart B as before, but beginning at
row 1.
Continue in this manner until body measures
12/13/14cm (4¾/5/5½in) from top of waist rib,
with right side facing for next row.

### RIGHT FRONT
Patt 30/33/34 sts. Place rem sts on a spare ndl.
Turn, and keeping continuity of patt, dec 1 st
at beg of next row (armhole edge).
Then decrease 1 st at armhole edge of next
and every foll alt row until 23/26/26 sts
remain.
Continue straight in patt until armhole
measures 8/8/9cm (3¼/3¼/3¾in), with wrong
side facing for next row.

### Shape neck
Patt to the last 5/6/6 sts. Place these sts on a
safety pin.
Next row: k2 tog, patt to end of row.
Keeping continuity of patt, decrease 1 st at
end of next row.
Patt 1 row straight, then decrease 1 st at end
(neck edge) of next and every foll alt row
until 13/14/14 sts remain.
Patt 1 row straight.

### Shape shoulder
With wrong side facing, cast off 6 sts, patt to
the last 2 sts, p2 tog.
Patt 1 row straight, then cast off rem 6/7/7 sts.

### BACK
With right side facing, rejoin yarn to the sts
on spare needle and cast off the next 6/6/7 sts
(right armhole), then keeping continuity of
patt, work the next 61/65/67 sts. Leave the
rem sts on the spare needle.
Turn, and decrease 1 st at each end of the
next 2 rows.
Patt 1 row straight, then decrease 1 st at each
end of next and every foll alt row until 47/51/
53 sts remain.
Continue straight in patt until back
corresponds in length with front at shoulder,
with right side facing for next row.

### Shape shoulders
Cast off 6 sts at beg of next 2 rows.
Cast of 6/7/7 sts at beg of next 2 rows.
Place the rem 23/25/27 sts on a length of yarn
for back neck.

### LEFT FRONT
With right side facing, rejoin yarn to the rem
sts on spare needle and cast off the next 6/6/7
sts (left armhole), then keeping continuity of
patt, work to end of row.
Turn and work the left front as right, but
reversing all shapings. **

### SLEEVES
With 3¼mm ndls and MS, cast on 29/30/32
sts.
K1, p1 rib for 4cm (1½in).

### Next row: increase
Rib 1/1/2, (m1, rib 2) to the last 2/1/1 sts; m1,
rib 2/1/1. 43/45/47 sts.
Change to 4mm ndls and work 2 rows st.st.
Work stripes as follows:
1 row 1st C/1 row 2nd C/2 rows MS.
Join in 1st C and work the patt from chart A,
repeating the 16 patt sts 2 times across, and

working the first 5/6/7 sts and the last 6/7/8 sts on k rows, and the first 6/7/8 sts and the last 5/6/7 sts on p rows as indicated.

Break off 1st C and with MS st.st. for 2 rows. Then joining in and breaking off colours as required, work the patt from chart B, beginning at row 15/7/3, and repeating the 6 patt sts 7 times across, and working the first 0/1/2 sts and the last 1/2/3 sts on k rows, and the first 1/2/3 sts and the last 0/1/2 sts on p rows as indicated.

Continue in this manner until sleeve measures approx 23/27/31cm (9/10½/12in) from beg, and ending on the *same* patt row as armhole cast off.

### *** Shape top

Keeping continuity of patt, cast off 3 sts at beg of next 2 rows.

Patt 2/2/4 rows straight, then decrease 1 st at each end of next and every foll alt row until 17/17/19 sts remain.

Then decrease 1 st at each end of next and every foll row until 7/7/9 sts remain.

Cast off the rem sts.

### FINISHING

To block and press see Guide to Techniques. Sew up inside leg seams.

Sew up crotch seam, beginning at centre back and stitching around front, leaving the front opening to measure 30cm (12in) from neck. Sew up shoulder seams. Sew up sleeve seams. Insert sleeves, placing centre top of sleeve at shoulder seam.

### Neck

With right side facing, 3¼mm needles, MS, and beginning at right neck, pick up and knit the 5/6/6 sts from safety pin, knit up 8/9/9 sts up right side, pick up and knit the 23/25/27 sts of back neck, decreasing 1 st at centre, knit up 8/9/9 sts down left side, and pick up and knit the 5/6/6 sts from safety pin. 48/54/56 sts.

Work border as follows:

Row 1: With MS, knit

Row 2: Knit 2/0/2 in MS, *k2 – 1st C, k2 – MS; rep from * to end of row

Row 3: As row 2 but bringing the yarns to the front of work

Row 4: With 1st C, Knit.

Cast off evenly in 1st C.

### Left front opening

With right side facing, 3¼mm needles, MS, and beginning at top of neck border, knit up 66 sts down left opening.

Knit 2 rows. Cast off evenly.

### Right front opening

With right side facing, 3¼mm needles and MS, knit up 66 sts up right opening.

Work border as follows:

Row 1: With MS, knit

Row 2: k2 – MS, * k2 – 1st C, k2 – MS; rep from * to end of row

Row 3: As row 2 but bringing yarns to front

Row 4: With 1st C – knit.

Cast off evenly in 1st C.

Insert zip so that right front border overlaps to cover.

Using 1 strand of each colour, make a cord and thread through waist eyelets.

To make cord see Guide to Techniques.

Thread beads on to each end of cord. ***

## CATSUIT (Short Version)

### RIGHT LEG

With 3¼mm needles and MS, cast on 58/62/66 sts.

K1, p1 rib for 2.5cm (1in).

### Next row: increase

Rib 0/0/2, (rib 3, m1) 6 times, (rib 2, m1) 11/13/13 times, (rib 3, m1) 6 times, rib 0/0/2. 81/87/91 sts.

Change to 4mm needles and work 2 rows in st.st.

Work stripes as follows:

1 row 1st C/1 row 2nd C/2 rows MS.

Join in 1st C and work the patt from chart A, repeating the 16 patt sts 5 times across, and working the first 0/3/5 sts and the last 1/4/6 sts on k rows, and the first 1/4/6 sts and the last 0/3/5 sts on p rows as indicated.

Break off 1st C, and with MS st.st. for 2 rows. Then joining in and breaking off colours as required, work the patt from chart B, repeating the 6 patt sts 13/14/15 times across, and working the first 1/1/0 sts and the last 2/2/1 sts on k rows, and the first 2/2/1 sts and the last 1/1/0 sts on p rows as indicated. Continue in this manner until leg measures 11/13/15cm (4¼/5/6in) from beg, with right side facing for next row.

Now work as long version from ** to **

N.B. work the left leg as right leg ending on the *same* patt row.

## SLEEVES

With 3¼mm needles and MS, cast on 32/34/36 sts.

K1, p1 rib for 2.5cm (1in).

**Next row: increase**

Rib 1/2/3, (m1, rib 3) 10 times, m1, rib 1/2/3. (43/45/47 sts).

Change to 4mm needles and work 2 rows in st.st.

Work stripes and chart A as sleeves of long version.

Then with MS, st.st for 2 rows.

Then joining in and breaking off colours as required, work the patt from chart B, repeating the 6 patt sts 7 times across, and working the first 0/1/2 sts and the last 1/2/3 sts on k rows, and the first 1/2/3 sts and the last 0/1/2 sts on p rows as indicated.

Work chart B until patt row matches the row before armhole cast off, and sleeve measures approx 9.5/10/11cm (3¾/4/4¼in) from beg.

Shape top of sleeve and finish catsuit as long version, from *** to ***.

# 8
# BACK TO THE PARLOUR

◇

# English Lace

Girl's blouse (ages 2–7)

*Little Indian, Sioux or Crow,*
*Little frosty Eskimo,*
*Little Turk or Japanee,*
*Oh don't you wish that you were me?*

*You have seen the scarlet trees*
*And the lions overseas;*
*You have eaten ostrich eggs,*
*And turned the turtles off their legs.*

*Such a life is very fine,*
*But it's not as nice as mine:*
*You must often as you trod,*
*Have wearied not to be abroad.*

*You must dwell beyond the foam,*
*But I am safe and live at home.*

Lace knitting – mainly in the form of samples – became a fashionable drawing room occupation during the time of Robert Louis Stevenson. This pretty blouse features the dewdrop pattern – a dainty and uncomplicated lace which is emphasised by the square shaping of the garment. Depending on the mood, ribbons may be run through the collar to create a softer effect.

## SIZES
Approx age: 2–3/4–5/6–7 years
To fit chest: 56/63/66cm (22/24/26in)
Length from top of shoulder: 34/38/42cm
(13½/15/16½in)
Sleeve seam: 18/21/24cm (7/8¼/9½in)

## YARN
3/4/4 1oz (28g) hanks of 2-ply Shetland lace
weight yarn
The yarn used in this garment is Jamieson &
Smith 2-ply Shetland lace weight yarn in
shade L53

## NEEDLES
1 pair 3mm needles

## NOTIONS
3 small buttons

## TENSION
17 sts and 22 rows to 5cm (2in), measured
over patt using 3mm needles.

## BACK
** With 3mm needles cast on 109/115/121 sts.
Work 7/7/9 rows garter stitch (k every row)
Now work main patt as follows:
Rows 1 and 3: (wrong side) k2, * p3, k3; rep
    from *, end p3, k2
Row 2: p2, * k3, p3; rep from *, end k3, p2
Row 4: k2, * yo, sl1–k2 tog–psso, yo, k3; rep
    from *, end yo, sl1–k2 tog–psso, yo, k2
Rows 5 and 7: p2, * k3, p3; rep from *, end
    k3, p2
Row 6: k2, * p3, k3; rep from *, end p3, k2
Row 8: k2 tog, * yo, k3, yo, sl1–k2 tog–psso;
    rep from *, end yo, k3, yo, ssk.
Repeat rows 1 to 8. ***
Continue in this manner until back measures
26/30/34cm (10½/12/13½in) from beg, with
right side facing for next row.

## Divide for back neck opening
Patt 54/57/60 sts. Place the rem sts on a spare
needle.
Turn, and keeping continuity of patt, work
these sts until piece measures 31.5/35.5/
39.5cm (12½/14/15½in), with wrong side facing
for next row.

## Shape right shoulder
Cast off the first 17/18/19 sts, patt the rem
37/39/41 sts.
Continue working these sts in patt for a
further 2cm (¾in), ending with right side
facing for next row.
Work 4 rows garter st. Place all sts on a spare
needle.
With right side facing, rejoin yarn to the 55/
57/61 sts of left side; cast off the first (centre
back) st, then patt to end of row.
Work these 54/57/60 sts as right side,
reversing shaping.

## FRONT
As back from ** to ***.
Continue in patt until front measures 28/31/
34.5cm (11/12¼/13½in) from beg, with right
side facing for next row.

## Shape left shoulder
Patt 37/39/41 sts. Place the rem sts on a spare
needle.
Turn, and keeping continuity of patt, work
these sts for a further 5.5/6.5/7cm (2¼/2½/2¾in),
ending with right side facing for next row.
Work 4 rows garter st. Place all sts on a spare
needle.

## Shape neck
With right side facing, rejoin yarn and cast off
the first (centre front) 35/37/39 sts; patt the
rem 37/39/41 sts.
Work these sts as left shoulder.

## SLEEVES
With 3mm needles, cast on 85/91/97 sts and

work 7/7/9 rows garter st.
Then work patt as back until sleeve measures 18/21/24cm (7/8¼/9½in) from beg, with right side facing for next row.
Work 4 rows garter st. Cast off all sts evenly.

## COLLAR

(Work 2 pieces alike)
With 3mm needles cast on 61/61/67 sts and work 5 rows garter st.
Then work patt as back until collar measures 5/5/5½cm (2/2/2¼in), with right side facing for next row.
Next row: Patt 17/16/18 sts. Place the rem sts on a spare needle.
Turn, and keeping continuity of patt, work these sts for a further 5/5/5½cm (2/2/2¼in) with right side facing for next row.
Work 3/5/5 rows garter st. Cast off all sts evenly.

### Shape neck

With right side facing, rejoin yarn and cast off the next (centre collar) 27/29/31 sts) patt the rem 17/16/18 sts.
Turn and work these sts as previous side.
With right side facing, knit up 20/19/21 sts along both ends of each collar.
Work 2/4/4 rows garter st.
Cast off evenly.

## FINISHING

With right sides of back and front together, cast off shoulder sts together from spare needles.
The individual pieces require no pressing as the dewdrop pattern produces a flat fabric.
Press all seams gently, as stated in Guide to Techniques.

### Attach collar

Pin each collar over neck edge so that centre cast off edges of collars fit along sides of neck.
Then with right side facing knit up 27/29/31 sts along neck edge, knitting up the sts

through both collar and neck edges, thus joining them.
Work 6 rows in garter st, decreasing 1 st at each end of first and every foll alt row. Cast off the rem 21/23/25 sts.
Pin front edges of collar along front neck edge so that the pieces meet at centre front.
With right side facing, knit up 35/37/39 sts along front neck edge, knitting through collar and neck edge as before.
Work 6 rows in garter st, decreasing 1 st at each end of first and every foll alt row. Cast off the rem 29/31/33 sts.
Pin each back collar piece over back neck edges so that collar pieces fit to back neck opening.
With right side facing, knit up 17/18/19 sts along back neck edge, knitting through collar and neck edge as before.
Work 6 rows garter st, decreasing 1 st at *end* of first and foll alt row for *right* back neck, and at *beg* of first and foll alt row for *left* back neck.
Cast off the rem 14/15/16 sts.

### Right back neck opening

With right side facing, knit up 24 sts along opening.
Work 4 rows garter st. Cast off evenly.

### Left back neck opening

With right side facing, knit up 24 sts along opening.
Work 1 row garter st.

### Next row: make buttonholes

K2, (k2 tog, yo, k7) twice, k2 tog, yo, k2.
Work 2 more rows garter st.
Cast off evenly.
Stitch down buttonhole edge over button edge.
Stitch garter st neck edges together at corners.
Place centre top of sleeve at shoulder seams and sew on sleeves.
Sew up side and sleeve seams.
Sew on buttons to correspond with buttonholes.

# Guide to Techniques

**FAIR ISLE**

This technique uses two colours in the same row, stranding or weaving the yarn not in use across the back of the work.

**STRANDING**

This method is used when not more than five stitches are worked in one colour. Holding the yarn in use with the right hand and the yarn not in use in the left hand, knit the required number of stitches in the first colour. Then carry the second colour *loosely* across the work, and knit the required number of stitches in this colour. (See Fig. 1)

On purl rows, the colour not in use is carried across the front of the work.

**WEAVING**

It is advisable to use this method when more than five stitches are worked in one colour, as weaving avoids long strands on the back of the work, which may catch and break.

Hold the yarns as for the stranding method and work the first stitch. Then on the next and every following third stitch, put the point of the right hand needle into the stitch, then carry the yarn in the left hand over the top of the right-hand needle, and knit the stitch with the yarn in the right hand in the usual way, thus catching the yarn not in use without working it. (See Fig. 2)

Weave the yarn in the same way on purl rows, across the front of the work, and

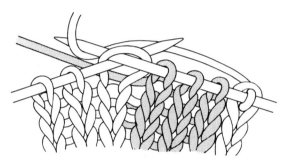

Fig. 1 Stranding

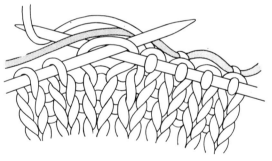

Fig. 2 Weaving

weaving in on the first and every following third stitch.

**FINISHING**

**Blocking and pressing**

Before pressing, check the instructions on the ball band (some man-made yarns should not be pressed).

126

If pressing is recommended, then each piece should be pinned out to size, right side down, on a flat surface e.g. a large table or the floor covered with blankets and ironing sheet. Use plenty of pins (approximately 4cm (1½in) apart), and make sure that the stitches and rows are straight, and the side edges are not pulled out of shape.

Have the iron at the recommended heat (warm for wool), and place a piece of cloth (damp for wool) over the pinned out piece. Omitting ribbing, press the whole surface with an up and down motion, i.e. lifting the iron up in the air, then placing it down on the knitting. Never use a sideways motion as this will stretch the knitting out of shape. Remove the cloth after pressing, and remove the pins when the piece has cooled.

## Seaming
Use the same or a finer matching yarn to make up the garment. For Fair Isle, use the predominant shade in the area being seamed. Use small even stitches so that seams will not show, and make sure that the pattern matches at the seams. Backstitch is recommended for seaming Fair Isle, and a loose, even catch stitch around necks and in areas where a little give is required. Press each seam lightly as you go along.

## JACQUARD
The Jacquard technique is used when the design consists of isolated areas in different colours. You use separate balls for each colour section, thus avoiding carrying the yarn across the back of the work. A fabric of single thickness is produced. When changing from one colour to another you must always cross the yarns, as follows:

## To cross yarns (right side rows)
Knit the required number of stitches with the first colour, then hold this colour to the left, at the back of the work. Then pick up the second colour and carry it to the right at the back of the work, under and over the strand

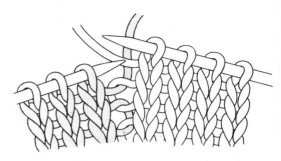

Fig. 3 Crossing yarns

of the first colour. Then work the required stitches with the second colour (see fig.3).

Work the wrong side rows in the same manner, crossing the yarns at the front of the work.

## Bobbins
When working a Jacquard design using several colours at once, make bobbins by cutting pieces of card, approx 8cm (3in) square, and winding on several yards of each colour. Make a small cut at one end of the cards and slip the yarn through this to stop it from unwinding.

## SWISS DARNING
Thread a tapestry needle with the contrast yarn and bring it through the work, from the back so that it comes out on the right side, at the base of the first stitch to be covered.

Then * Insert the needle from right to left, under the 2 threads of the stitch immediately above the stitch to be covered. Then take it through to the wrong side at the base of the stitch being covered, i.e. the starting point. Then bring it out at the base of the next stitch to be covered. Repeat from *.

## CORDS
Cut two lengths of yarn, approximately four times the desired length of the finished cord. Knot the ends together. You will now need the help of another person.

Insert a pencil at each end of front of knot, between lengths of yarn. Facing each other, and holding the yarn together between finger and thumb, in front of pencil, turn pencils clockwise until strands are tightly twisted. Bring pencils together and allow the cord to twist. Remove the pencils and knot the end of the cord.

**POMPOMS**
Cut two pieces of card into a circle, giving the finished size of the pompom. Then cut a smaller circle in the centre of each card (the size of this hole should about a quarter of the finished pompom).

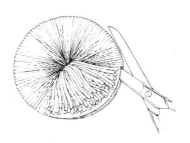

Fig. 4 Pompoms

Thread a darning needle with a long length of doubled yarn. With the two pieces of card together, wind the yarn evenly round and through the centre hole until it is filled. Cut through the yarn at the outer edge, between the cards. (See Fig. 4)

Tie a length of yarn tightly round the middle of the pompom, between the cards, leaving enough yarn to sew the pompom to the cord. Remove the cards and trim the pompom to give a good, round shape.

YARN SUPPLIERS

Jamieson & Smith Ltd., 90 North Road, Lerwick, Shetland.

R. V. Marriner Ltd., Knowle Mills, South Street, Keighley, W. Yorks, BD21 1DW

Emu Wools, Leeds Road, Greengates, Bradford.

Pinguoin, French Wools Ltd., 7–11 Lexington Street, London, W1R 5BU.

Hayfield Textiles Ltd., Hayfield Mills, Glusburn, Keighley, W. Yorks, BD20 8QP.